That Voice Behind You

That Voice Behind You

Charles G. Coleman

LOIZEAUX BROTHERS

Neptune, New Jersey

First Edition, May 1977
Revised Edition, January 1991

That Voice Behind You: God's Guidance in Daily
Decisions
© 1977 Loizeaux Brothers, Inc.
© 1991 Charles G. Coleman

A publication of Loizeaux Brothers, Inc.
a nonprofit organization devoted to the Lord's
work and to the spread of His truth.

Printed in the United States of America.

Library of Congress Cataloging-in-Publication
Data
Coleman, Charles G.
    That voice behind you: God's guidance in
daily decisions/Charles G. Coleman.—Rev.
ed.
        p. cm.
    Rev. ed. of: Divine guidance, that voice
behind you.
    Includes bibliographical references.
    ISBN 0-87213-087-8
    1. Christian life—1960- 2. God—Will.
    I. Coleman, Charles G.
    Divine guidance, that voice behind you. II. Title.
    BV4501.2.C6355   1991
    248.4—dc20   90-46238

Note to the Reader: Portions of this book originally
appeared in *Divine Guidance: That Voice Behind You.*
The current edition has been substantially revised
and updated.

Scripture quotations unless otherwise stated are
taken from the *Holy Bible, New International Version.*
Copyright © 1973, 1978, 1984 International Bible
Society. Used by permission of Zondervan Bible
Publishers.

10 9 8 7 6 5 4 3 2 1

This book
is dedicated to
Linda, Steve, and Becky
daughters and son
who are also
close and valued friends.

W hether you turn to
the right or to the left,
your ears will hear a
voice behind you, say-
ing, "This is the way;
walk in it."

Isaiah 30:21

Contents

CHAPTER 1

What Do You Know for Sure?

Does God guide men and women today? Before we try to answer this question, we must first consider a more basic one. Is God (whoever He may be) interested in the personal lives of human beings? • Most of you who read this believe that there is a God who created the universe, or at least started things off. You may also agree that this God is all-wise and all-powerful, and that He has some sort of master plan for the world. But you may not be sure what the plan is, or how He controls things to bring it about. • Maybe you have been discouraged because of the injustice and suffering you've seen, and suspect that God is a great impersonal life force of some sort that doesn't care about you. Or maybe you are convinced that God has set up life as a kind of obstacle course, with prizes or punishments waiting at the end. • Whatever your idea of God, you may wonder about His role in the world, because the world picture seems so mixed up, and because it contains so much that is evil. "Where is God anyway?" you ask. "If He is in charge, why doesn't He straighten out these problems?"

God: Alive or Dead?

Before scientific discovery stripped so much of the mystery from the activities of nature, it was easier for people, whether Christians or not, to think of God as taking a direct, daily interest in human affairs. Rain, wind, and sunshine were commonly considered to be specific "acts of God" (language which persists in our present-day insurance policies). It was God who made vegetables and fruits to flourish, and who allowed famine to come. Scientific progress, by providing natural explanations for many things previously mysterious, has, bit by bit, changed the popular conception of God. It has made Him seem more remote, and it gives to those who want to do away with Him altogether an opportunity to do so. "God was really just a 'gap-filler,'" says the atheist. "He was needed to account for the things men didn't know how to explain. Now that science has given us better explanations, we can consider that God is dead."

I am not saying, of course, that modern science has proven the atheists' case for them or even that it lends support. In the view of a number of thinking people, including many competent scientists, atheism can't provide a satisfactory explanation of the great problem of life's origin. Christianity does. Dr. Jack Wood Sears, biologist, put it this way: "The Bible has answered man's most important questions. From whence did I come? Where am I going? . . . Science has no answers to these questions" (97). Dr. Owen Gingerich, astrophysicist at the Smithsonian Observatory, wrote, "The power of Genesis 1 as God's revelation will survive long after the slide rule science of our age is outmoded, abandoned or forgotten" (Bube 133).

Even the Christian's view of God, however, has been affected by the advance of science. Before the rise of modern science, most Christians believed that the creator brought the world into existence in its present form through an instant miracle a few thousand years ago. While some hold this view today, others are inclined to accept the idea that the earth's history extends back for millions of years. And while Christians realize that the Bible itself does not say when (or even exactly how) the work of creation was done, they are likely to feel that the God who presided over the ice ages and dinosaurs and the slow erosion of the Grand Canyon is a different sort of deity from the one pictured in their earliest Sunday school books.

If you are a young person, science may pose a special problem for you. You may want to struggle free from what seem to you to be the unscientific views of the older generation and, at the same time, to find a real relationship with God. In your struggle, you find that you are unsure as to which of the ideas of the older generations you should throw away, and which you should keep. You may also have difficulty fitting together what you have been taught as a child about God's love, His care for you, and His daily guidance, and some of the scientific explanations of life and the universe that seem to move Him out of the picture entirely.

Whatever your age, any doubts you have about God may be increased as you come in contact with people who attend church regularly, quote the Bible, and claim to be in daily communion with God, but whose real interests seem to be centered more on their homes and cars and televisions than on doing God's will. When you see the difference between what Christian teaching *says*, and what many who profess to be Christians *do*, you are likely to wonder whether or not God is really concerned with the daily lives of individual human beings.

You may be tempted to conclude that the whole idea of people getting practical guidance from God is just another fairy story from the past—a relic of the centuries of ignorance when men thought that thunder was the literal voice of God, and looked for omens in the entrails of pigeons.

What the Bible Says

Against these problems, let us place the Bible. The Bible promises that God will guide us if we want His guidance. I have found these promises to be true, but I do not recommend that you take my word for this. I suggest that you investigate the matter of divine guidance for yourself. Any such investigation must begin with the Bible.

The natural universe, which science explores, was designed by God and testifies to His wisdom, but nature alone cannot tell us how He deals with individual human beings. Our observations of other people are not always reliable indicators. (Other Christians can help us to understand God, but looking at someone else's solution to a problem can sometimes give us the wrong answer.)

God has, however, given us His word, the Bible, to illuminate our way (Psalm 119:105). It is through our study of the scriptures and the working of the Holy Spirit in our individual lives that we learn what God is really like.

The Bible tells us a great deal about God's purposes. It pictures the world as a great battleground in the struggle between good and evil, a struggle in which human beings are key elements. Through humanity, the Bible explains, sin became dominant in the world. And it was when God Himself became man, in the person of Jesus Christ, that the climax of the struggle was reached. By dying on the cross and rising again Jesus destroyed the power of sin forever (Hebrews 2:14).

When men and women, by a process called "faith," receive the risen Christ into their lives as their Savior and Lord, they become Christians. Becoming a Christian, in the sense in which the Bible uses the term, means becoming a child of God, a member of His family.

God's promises to give daily care and guidance are for His own family. Therefore, if you have never recognized your need of Christ and received Him as your personal Savior, you have no right to expect God to guide you in life's problems. Once you have become His child, however, you belong to Him forever. Just as conscientious human parents provide for their children, your heavenly Father stands ready to care for and guide you.

If you are not yet a member of God's family, you must begin this journey at the starting point. For your life to have real meaning, you must be set free from sin and evil and put in contact with God. To become a child of God you must come to Jesus Christ, recognize that He died on the cross for you, and accept Him into your life as Lord and Savior (John 5:24). Then and only then will you be able to tune in to God's daily guidance.

How to Begin

What if you are one of those who are not sure that God cares about you? Let me point you to something Jesus said. He was often confronted by those whose attitude was, "Prove to us that you really represent God; then we will decide whether or not to do what you say." On one occasion, Jesus responded by reversing the order of these two ideas. He said, "If anyone chooses to do God's will, he will find out whether my teaching comes from God or whether I speak on my own" (John 7:17). This statement makes it clear that God is not in the business of satisfying idle curiosity. He will reveal Himself, but only to sincere seekers—those who are interested in doing His will.

If you truly want to find God, speak to Him even though you are not sure that He is listening. Tell Him that if He gives you assurance that He is real, you are ready to commit your life to Him. Then begin reading the Bible (one of the gospels is a good place to start). If you approach the scriptures with this attitude, your study will lead you to a conviction that God exists and to an understanding of the Bible message. The subject of God's guidance will then become meaningful.

If you are already a Christian but you are not now taking advantage of the daily guidance God wants to give you, this book will, I hope, point the way to a new, exciting way of living the Christian life.

What I have tried to do in the following pages is to present, as simply and clearly as possible, what God tells us in the scriptures about His will and how it works. If you begin your study with an open mind, a determination to find out what the Bible itself has to say, and a willingness to give what you learn about God's will a chance in your life, you can be certain that God will show you through His word how to make that life worthwhile.

QUESTIONS

1. How have scientific discoveries made over the centuries changed the popular conception of God?

2. What do some atheists mean when they suggest that God was a "gap-filler"?

3. What are some fundamental questions about the human race that the Bible answers, but science does not?

4. What are two resources that can help you understand what God is like?

5. If, as this chapter says, the world is a battleground, what are the opposing forces, and by what great act was the outcome decided?

6. According to the Bible, how does one become a Christian?

7. What does John 5:24 indicate happens to those who believe?

8. What kind of "life" is this verse talking about?

9. How can John 7:17 be of help to those who have honest doubts as to whether or not God exists?

10. How does the fact that Christianity involves a "family relationship" help you to understand God's daily guidance?

CHAPTER 2

Some Basic Questions

Nearly four thousand years ago in Egypt, a young ruler faced his brothers. Long ago they had done him a terrible wrong, and they now feared that he would use his power to avenge himself. "Don't be afraid," Joseph reassured them. "You intended to harm me but God intended it for good" (Genesis 50:19-20). • Now shift your historical telescope forward to a mere twenty-five hundred years ago. In the royal palace of Persia, a beautiful young queen was asked by her uncle to undertake a dangerous mission. She was to use her influence to reverse a decision made by the king, her husband, and thus change Persian national policy. Her task was an important one, for the lives of the entire Jewish population were at stake. But if she tried and failed, she would almost certainly lose her life. Her uncle urged her to make the attempt. "Who knows but that you have come to royal position for such a time as this?" he said (Esther 4:14). Queen Esther nodded in agreement. Boldly she entered the king's presence to present her case. She was successful and her people were saved. • Come farther forward still. Some nineteen hundred years ago, a physician named Luke recorded his experiences as a member of a traveling evangelistic team. As they journeyed through what is now Turkey, their leader, the great apostle Paul, saw in a night vision a man who begged him to sail westward to the Macedonian peninsula. Luke wrote, "We got ready at once to leave for Macedonia, concluding that God had called us to preach the gospel to them" (Acts 16:10).

Through these stories runs a common thread. The individuals, living as they did in different cultural settings, and separated in time by centuries, shared a common conviction that God was concerned with the details of their daily lives. His will was an active force with which they must reckon, and to which they should respond. Joseph was willing to forgive his brothers because he discerned the hand of God in the circumstances that their malicious deed had brought about. Queen Esther risked her life because she believed that God had a special role for her to play in the affairs of the nation. Paul modified his travel plans because he recognized that God was planning his itinerary.

For those who accept the Bible as God's word, these and other similar incidents provide strong evidence that God stands ready to guide those who are willing to accept His guidance. But such incidents do not, in themselves, answer all the questions people ask about God's will. Let's look at some of these questions:

The discussions I have heard about God's will seem to get involved in terminology. What do you mean by "God's will"?

It is true that people who write about God's will often begin by dividing the subject into categories. To these they assign titles such as "God's sovereign will," "God's permissive will," "God's intentional will," "God's directive will," and "God's moral will." None of these terms is found in scripture, and each writer seems to have his own set.

In most cases these terms refer, not to divisions within God's will, but to the ways in which this will is expressed or accomplished. Thus when God does things in spite of human opposition, He is said to exercise His "sovereign will." To some the term, "God's moral will," means God's commands as recorded in the Bible. "God's permissive will" comes into play when He allows a rebellious follower to do something other than what God wants him to do.

If you find such terms useful, by all means keep them. However, they can also be confusing. While we will see, later on, some variations in the way God's purposes are carried out under different conditions, in this book we will think of God's will as being simply what He wants to have done at any given time.

If God's will is what He wants done, why does He hold man responsible when things go wrong? Doesn't God have the power to control everything?

Yes, He does. The Bible gives us examples of the operation of God's will in human affairs. Nowhere is this better illustrated than in the first six chapters of the book of Daniel. There we see, in a series of spectacular incidents, the will of God in action in the greatest empire of that age. Nebuchadnezzar, ruler of most of the known world, after seeing the evidence of God's power, said: "He does as he pleases with the powers of heaven and the peoples of the earth. No one can hold back his hand or say to him: 'What have you done?'"(Daniel 4:35). We find, repeated three times over, the assertion: "The Most High is sovereign over the kingdoms of men, and gives them to anyone he wishes" (Daniel 4:17,25,32).

While God's hand in world affairs is not always as visible as it was in Daniel's time, the scriptures teach that in every age He works all things "in conformity with the purpose of his will" (Ephesians 1:11). In other words, God is in control.

However, in the world around us we see constant evidence of man's will in action, and the Bible also talks about the freedom people have to decide things for themselves. There are, for example, the well-known words of Joshua to the Israelites, "Choose for yourselves this day whom you will serve . . . But as for me and my household, we will serve the Lord" (Joshua 24:15). Many other scripture texts confirm that any person is at liberty to refuse God. As a result, tyrants like Hitler, acting ruthlessly and in self-will, can throw the world into war and bring suffering to many. Because they have freedom of choice, such men are responsible for their acts.

Well then, who is in charge, anyway, God or man?

Let's go back to the beginning. God created human beings with the right of self-determination, and the authority to rule the earth (Genesis 1:26). I believe that, in so doing, God voluntarily restricted His own sovereignty. In other words, on this planet, a tiny part of the domain of God, the Almighty chose to limit Himself in order to allow men and women to exercise their own freedom of choice.

Humans could have ruled this earth successfully if they had followed God's laws and leaned on God's wisdom and aid. But self-determination included the right to choose not to listen to God. When Adam and Eve sinned, they lost control of their world. And God, His sabbath rest broken, worked unceasingly through the subsequent ages, bringing His great plan of redemption to fruition in the midst of the chaos caused by His creatures.

When the Lord Jesus was accused of breaking the sabbath by healing the sick, He replied simply, "My Father is always at his work to this very day, and I, too, am working" (John 5:17). In the phrase, "to this very day," we can glimpse the great panorama of time from Genesis to Matthew during which the master planner labored. He appealed to people of every age through nature, through the human conscience, and through prophets and teachers. He guided the course of empires to provide Himself a witness in the world, and to arrange for the coming of His Son, who was to attack sin at its root and destroy it. As He did so, God was careful not to violate the right of self-determination He had given. He will not force men and women to believe in Him, to keep His laws, or to obey His directives.

That explanation is all right as far as it goes, but how is it that God is able to carry out His purposes in the world without interfering with our freedom of choice?

The Bible does not give us a precise formula, but it does give us definite clues to God's methods. Let's look, for example, at the process of individual salvation as described in the scriptures.

John's gospel states that "whoever believes" has everlasting life (John 3:16). Many other verses confirm that the decision to believe in Christ is ours to make. But the Bible also teaches that God chose those who believe "before the foundation of the world" (Ephesians 1:4). Here is an apparent contradiction.

The apostle Paul resolved this puzzle beautifully in Romans 8:28-30, and in so doing gave us an idea of how God fits the pieces of our lives together:

> And we know that in all things God works for the good of those who love him, who have been called according to his purpose. For those God foreknew he also predestined to be conformed to the likeness of his Son, that he might be the firstborn among many brothers. And those he predestined, he also called; those he called, he also justified; those he justified, he also glorified.

Notice the sequence of these statements:

1. God "foreknows." Some interpret the word *foreknow* to mean "foreordained" or "predetermined," and some modern language paraphrases follow this interpretation. However, there is no reason why the word should not mean simply "to know in advance," and I interpret it in this sense. The message, then, is that God knows ahead of time who is going to accept His Son as Savior.

2. God "predestinates." This means that He ordains or decrees ahead of time, not that one person should be saved and another lost, but that the person who does believe will be conformed or changed into the image of His Son. This change for the better begins in our lives when we accept Christ as our Savior, and is finally completed when we finish our lives here and join Him in heaven.

3. God "calls," "justifies," "glorifies." These are the steps God takes to carry out the plan of salvation for the one whose acceptance He foreknew. While God's salvation is sufficient for everyone, those who do not respond to the gospel are not predestined for the good things that follow, because it is foreknown that they will not accept God's offer.

Suppose a company employing one thousand people holds an annual free picnic for its employees. As a result of many years' experience, the planners predict that fewer than six hundred will attend, although the invitation is given to all. This prediction can be considered a sort of "foreknowledge." On the strength of this information, the company arranges for enough buses to transport six hundred people to the picnic site, buys six hundred portions of food, and plans activities on the basis of the six hundred it expects to attend.

Does this mean that the offer to the other four hundred is not real? Not at all. The decision not to attend is their own, freely made. However, if the company knows in advance that some will not attend, it would be foolish to make preparations for them.

God, through His foreknowledge, knows not only the number but the identity of each person who will receive Jesus Christ as Savior. Even though the salvation He has provided is enough for all, and offered freely to everyone, He has chosen to prearrange (or predestine) the good things that follow salvation for those who He knows will come to Him.

Some scholars hold a different view of foreknowledge, predestination, and the entire relationship between God's sovereignty and human will, from the one presented here. These differences are discussed in Note 1, at the end of this book.

Wait a minute! Doesn't God sometimes decide who will obey Him? For example, didn't He harden pharaoh's heart?

Yes, He did, as Exodus 4:21 tells us. This is a difficult passage to explain, and it is one of the reasons for the differences mentioned above. However I don't believe God's treatment of pharaoh necessarily contradicts what we have said. Let's look together at Romans 9:10-24.

Here, Paul moved his argument to the broad arena of world history. At first look, his reasoning seems to have little in common with that of chapter 8. In Romans 9:18-20 Paul stated that God can do exactly as He wishes in the world, and you and I have no right to question Him.

To illustrate his point, Paul gave two examples of God's intervention in the lives of men: first, the choice of Jacob, over his older brother Esau, to be the father of the nation of Israel (Genesis 25:23); and second, the destruction of pharaoh, the tyrannical king of Egypt who was drowned in the Red Sea (Exodus 9:16; 14:8,27). In both of these cases, God announced in advance what would happen to the individuals concerned, and then brought it about.

Paul's explanation? Simply that God may, if He wishes, and because He is God, choose to show mercy to some and to judge others. If this sounds to you as though Paul were defending God's right to be arbitrary, you are getting exactly the impression the apostle wanted you to get. He rejected in advance any objections you might raise by saying in effect, "Who do you think you are, anyway, to criticize God?"

One reason you and I have trouble understanding this chapter is that we forget that the book of Romans is really a letter, intended to be read at one sitting. What Paul wrote at the beginning, he expected his readers to remember as they read the rest.

In the first three chapters of Romans the apostle affirmed that God deals equally and impartially with all men. His grace, love, and salvation are for everyone (Romans 1:16; 2:11; 3:21-24). What I think Paul was doing in Romans 9 was "balancing the boat." Having told us some facts about God, he was now telling us something about ourselves. Paul's point was that, as sinful human creatures, we have neither the ability nor the right to judge almighty God. We have been assured that God is fair and just, and it is our responsibility to believe this. We cannot decide how God should deal with any individual.

However, if we carry over what we have learned about God's methods of operation from Romans 8, and apply it to the two cases in chapter 9, we find that it fits. Paul, you see, didn't say that Esau and pharaoh were forced to rebel—only that God chose Jacob over Esau before Esau's sins were committed, and that pharaoh was "raised up" to a position of prominence where his rebellion could trigger the departure of Israel from Egypt. If we begin with the truth that God loves all men, we can recognize in His "hate" for Esau simply His divine abhorrence of Esau's life of sin. His "hardening" of pharaoh's heart describes the inevitable effect of God's revelation on a man who rejects it. In both cases, the sequence of

God's foreknowledge followed by His action can account for the facts.

Suppose, for example, that the man who was pharaoh had been born into any one of the other thousands of families in Egypt. While he would have rejected the claims of God just as forcefully, his act would have had no effect on history. By seeing to it that he became king, God used his rejection to move Israel out of Egypt and toward the promised land.

God's job sounds rather complicated. Do we know what methods He uses in getting His purpose accomplished?

In later chapters I'll discuss some means God uses to guide Christians. I will not, in this book, describe the many ways by which He controls events in the world at large. It is well to remember, however, that the two processes are different.

We have already seen how God used His foreknowledge and power to place the Egyptian ruler in a position where his actions would further God's purposes. A similar example of God's power over nations is found in Isaiah 10:5-16, where He reveals to the prophet His plan to use the selfish ambition of an Assyrian monarch to deal with the nation of Israel. God also controls the powers of nature. The authority to rule the earth, which He gave to the human race in Genesis 1:26, did not include control of sunshine and rain, seasonal changes, famines, and earthquakes. These remain in the hand of God, and are used by Him as tools to accomplish His will.

Remember the stories about the cattle drives of the American west? Each drive was under a "trailmaster" who, with his men, rode the perimeter, nudging the herd slowly along. The individual animal in the middle of the mass was seldom conscious of the control exercised by the men, and was at liberty to graze, grumble, or fight as he wished. In spite of this freedom, the herd was moved steadily along the route decreed by the man in charge. While not a perfect metaphor, this illustration may suggest how God uses circumstances to influence world events. The cowboy uses his knowledge of how cattle respond to noise and pressure to move them along, as God uses His divine foreknowledge in controlling events.

God's will applied to the Christian suggests a different sort of mental image. While God controls the circumstances that surround His people, He also gives them the privilege of doing His will voluntarily. Christians can therefore expect God to communicate His wishes to them. To illustrate this relationship, let's picture a giant choir under the direction of an expert leader. Each member sings his own part and, by keeping his eye on the choir director, is able to contribute in a useful way to the grand plan of the oratorio.

As followers of God, we must recognize our responsibility to respond in an intelligent way to His direction as the vocalist does to the choir leader. Just as the singer must know what is expected of him in each piece, we must understand what it is God wants us to do. If we do not understand His will, we feel like inept members of the choral group, singing away in the back row some half-learned bit of the bass or alto, trying to keep ourselves on key by listening to our neighbors on each side, and squinting at the distant figure of the leader without being really certain just when he wants us to come in and when to remain silent.

I find it hard to understand why God works in these round-about ways. Since He is omnipotent, why doesn't He do away with evil entirely?

To this and other questions about why God does things, the answer is simply that He hasn't told us. The Bible answers most of our "how" questions about God's activities, but few of our "why" questions. However, since the problem of evil bothers all of us at one time or another, let's consider what we know about it.

One point the Bible makes emphatically is that, while God fits the actions of even rebellious lives into His worldwide purposes, He does not will or desire this rebellion. We read, for example, that God "wants all men to be saved, and to come to a knowledge of the truth" (1 Timothy 2:4). In simple terms, this means that God is doing all He can, within the limits He has established, to reach and save people. Since not everyone chooses to come to God, it is evident that God's will for every individual is not being done. People can reject Him, for this is a matter in which God permits man's will to be supreme. God's power to redeem and save is like the potential energy of water in a pipe, which can act only when a human hand turns the faucet.

We must also recognize that the possibility of evil is always present in a free will arrangement. Thus our God-given freedom to decide has to include the freedom to reject God and to do evil, even when this evil hurts other people. While God can, through circumstances, influence the course of a battle, He would be untrue to the rules of life if He forcibly restrained every individual who decided to shoot at someone else.

If you ask, "Then why doesn't God just terminate our free will and make us all do what is right?" you are posing, in effect, the unanswerable question: "Why are we people and not something else?"

Some refuse to believe in a God who allowed sin to come into the world in the first place, or who now permits wars and suffering to go on. This is, of course, their right. However, by taking this position, they are actually saying: "If I were God, and had His power and foreknowledge, I would banish evil and stop all suffering right away. Since if God existed, He would view the world as I do, and since pain and suffering continue, my conclusion is that there is no God." The fallacy of this reasoning is that God does not necessarily think as we do (Isaiah 55:8-9). God is, by definition, wiser than we are and, as we have seen in Romans 9, we cannot call Him to account.

While it may be necessary to give a three-year-old boy a medical injection, it isn't likely that the youngster himself can understand why the shot is needed. He accepts the discomfort because he trusts his parents when they tell him it is necessary. In the same way, it is unreasonable to expect everything God does to be perfectly comprehensible to the limited creatures He created. If you and I sincerely want to know God, He has promised to give us ample assurance of His existence, His presence, and His love. But we must be willing to trust Him to run the universe in His own way.

Finally, let's look at the entire question from another angle. The existence of evil is a fact. People have recognized it, and struggled against it, through the centuries, but have never been able to overcome it. The Bible offers us an explanation of how evil began, what God is doing about it, and how He will finally destroy it. If we reject the God of the Bible, we haven't solved the problem of evil. We are left, in fact, with no explanation at all.

Rejection of the Bible account can lead us to the gray land of agnosticism, with its conclusion that ultimate truth is unknowable, or to the even more bleak world of atheism, where good, evil, and life itself are essentially meaningless.

QUESTIONS

1. What is the common thread that connects the incidents involving Joseph, Esther, and Paul at the beginning of this chapter?

2. How is it suggested in this chapter that you define the phrase "God's will"?

3. Since God has the power to control everything, why does He hold human beings responsible for their actions?

4. Does Romans 8:29 teach that God predestines one person to be saved and another to be eternally condemned? If not, what does *predestination* mean?

5. In the illustration of the picnic, what elements correspond to the factors of foreknowledge, predestination, and free will?

6. In Romans 9:10-24, the examples of Esau and pharaoh are used to show that God has a right to act in a sovereign way. How does what you have learned about Romans 8 help you to understand God's dealings with these two men? How do Romans 1:16; 2:11; 3:21-24 help us to understand Romans 8 and 9?

7. How do the illustrations of the cattle drive and the choir used in this chapter relate to the two different kinds of control described in Psalm 32:8-9?

8. What statements in scripture suggest that, while God uses rebellious humans to further His purposes, He does not will or desire their rebellion?

9. What are some possible reasons why God has not done away with evil entirely?

10. What should your attitude be about this and other questions for which there are no certain answers?

CHAPTER 3

God's Will and You

The Bible says that Christians should be filled with the knowledge of God's will (Colossians 1:9). It must also be true that it is important for us to know God's will and that He has made it possible for us to do so. These truths raise some additional questions: • **Does God have a plan for my life, and will He guide me so that I can carry it out? If so, how much guidance can I expect Him to provide?** • You can find several different answers to these questions as you leaf through current books on guidance, and it is a good idea to face the fact of these differences. Before attempting to give my own answers, let's look at two concepts of guidance proposed by others. • The first of these, which has been widely taught for many years, we will call the "traditional view." Proponents of this view teach that God has an individual master plan for your life and that His guidance is designed to fit you into this plan. God's plan covers the major decisions: your choice of college, vocation, marriage partner, and so on. Traditionalists believe it is important that you seek God's guidance for every significant decision in life, though not necessarily for the less significant daily choices.

The traditional view has a healthy emphasis on dedication to God. It teaches the need for prayer and committing of important decisions to Him. It stresses the need to be sure choices are made in His will. It also warns of the danger of ignoring His guidance. If you fail to follow God's guidance in a major matter, such as marrying the wrong person, or failing to answer God's call to the missionfield, you may, according to this view, miss out on God's plan, and have to settle for a second-best Christian life.

Those who teach the traditional concept emphasize this danger. G. Christian Weiss expressed this view when he wrote of Christians who "have gone past that single entrance into the channel of His [God's] perfect will." For them, he said, "Life can never be the way He originally intended it." And he concluded, "It is a tragedy to miss the perfect will of God for one's life. Christian, mark well these words and this testimony, lest you too miss His first choice" (17).

While there is much that is biblical in the traditional view, critics have noted that there is little evidence in scripture to suggest that God's plan for the Christian life is a single unchangeable blueprint, or that failure dooms one to a second-best life. On the contrary, the concern of Bible writers seems to be that we should confess our mistakes to God, and learn from them, so that we can serve Him more wisely.

There are also practical difficulties with the traditional view. The possibility of making a tragic mistake has created tensions, particularly for those young in the faith. Some have agonized over which decision was the "right" one, and once a choice was made, lived in fear that they might have missed God's best, after all.

For these reasons, the last few decades have seen a swing away from the traditional view toward interpretations that are less rigorous. At the far end of this pendulum swing are those who believe that God does not have a specific plan for your life, but that you are free to develop your own plan. They teach that God's guidance comes to you only through the moral truths set forth in the Bible. Within this framework God adopts a hands-off policy. He expects you to follow your preferences in making decisions. Occasionally God may, for reasons of His own, want you to be at a certain place or perform some specific act. If so, He will govern your actions without your volition through His control of circumstances.

This concept achieved a certain modest popularity in the 1960s. More recently, it has been ably and persuasively expounded in the book, *Decision Making and the Will of God*, by Garry Friesen and J. Robin Maxson. The following words are their own partial summary of the teaching:

> In those areas specifically addressed by the Bible, the revealed commands and principles of God (His moral will) are to be obeyed.
> In those areas where the Bible gives no command or principle (non-moral decisions), the believer is free and responsible to choose his own course of action. Any decision made within the moral will of God is acceptable to God (257).

These authors are careful to state that you must, as a Christian, make decisions wisely. However, the message is clear that God doesn't care in most cases where you decide to live, what career you follow, and what marriage partner you choose. In each of these situations, any reasonable choice is the "right" one.

There are attractive aspects to this concept of guidance. It relieves its followers of the tensions inherent in the traditional view, it affirms the importance of following biblical principles, and it promotes a non-mystical, commonsense approach to decision making. However, many Christians find it hard to reconcile this teaching with the strong emphasis on practical guidance found throughout the Bible.

Some also find it less than comfortable in practice. You are encouraged in scripture to walk closely with God, and to seek His help in matters of practical as well as spiritual concern. Yet, under this new concept, you can no longer pray, "Lord, guide me in making this difficult decision," and expect Him to do so. When decision times come, you must now visualize Him, so to speak, stepping aside and watching silently as you struggle to find a solution.

These views are certainly far apart. How can people study the same Bible and come out with such different ideas?

When competent and respected teachers of the scriptures differ, it usually means that the matter is a difficult one to resolve. The subject of guidance is one of these difficult cases. It is important for you, the reader, to be aware of the difficulty, as you consider what this book has to say on the subject. In studying any Bible truth, it is helpful to read more than one exposition and then, following the good example of the Bereans of Acts 17:11, examine the scriptures for yourself, checking each view against what the Bible says before deciding on a final answer. In this case I believe the truth lies between these two extremes.

Okay. What is your view of guidance?

It can be summarized in the following three points:

1. While there is no one scripture passage which states that God has a detailed plan for your life, the Bible as a whole gives evidence that He does. This plan is not the unchangeable one of the traditional view, but a more flexible one that takes into account the mistakes which He knows you will make.

2. God desires to guide you in the many decisions, large and small, which you make each day, whether or not these decisions involve moral principles. His guidance comes through the Bible, and in other ways, which we will discuss later.

3. God does not want you to stand paralyzed before life's choices, waiting for special signs, but to make decisions promptly and confidently. His guidance, properly understood, is designed to help you do this.

Can you give me some reasons why you think God guides in non-moral, as well as moral decisions?

Let's begin with the Bible examples of divine guidance. Remember the examples of practical guidance we talked about in the last chapter? There are many other such incidents in scripture. In the Old Testament, Abraham, Moses, Gideon, David, and the prophets come to mind. In the New Testament, check what the Bible says about Philip, Peter, Cornelius, the prophet Ananias (who was told to visit Saul), the elders of the church at Antioch (who sent out Barnabas and Saul as missionaries), and the apostle Paul himself (who was guided in his travel by God).

If you believe God's guidance involves only moral matters, and comes only through scripture, you must dismiss all these cases of God's direction as special ones. Yet there is no indication that they were exceptions to the rule, and the fact that they are recorded for us in such numbers suggests otherwise.

Many Christians who lived during the centuries since the apostles walked the earth have found that God's guidance is both real and practical.

One striking example is the case of missionary Cyril Brooks, who with his wife Anna went to the Philippine Islands in the 1920s. This couple was used mightily by God in helping to open those islands to the gospel. Cyril recorded what happened when as a young man he prayed for guidance regarding his area of service: "It seemed as if the Lord said to me, 'Go to the Philippines.' I didn't even know where the Philippines were." Cyril said nothing to Anna, his wife-to-be, about this unusual experience. However, a short time later she was independently given assurance that she should go to this place as well. Subjective evidence? Yes, but to Cyril and Anna Brooks it was solid truth, which the Lord used later on to encourage them when they needed assurance. As a result of major hardships during their early years they were tempted to return home. "It would have been easy to become a missionary drop-out," Brooks wrote. "But we had this assurance that the Lord had sent us there with clear and definite guidance. Therefore, we would need equally clear guidance if He should want us to leave" (57-59).

Many other missionaries have heard the Lord's call clearly, though not all in the same way. For some, the steps were learning of a need, recognizing their fitness to fill that need, becoming convinced gradually but surely that this place of need was where God wanted them to serve, and having God confirm their call through other means. The common denominator was the conviction in all these cases that God had guided. The pioneer African missionary T. Ernest Wilson summarized God's role in the process when he wrote, "The sovereign Lord is the One who calls, prepares and sends the servant, and shows him the task he is to perform" (3).

How about your claim that God guides all my decisions, large and small? Did you really mean that? After all, some of the decisions I make are rather insignificant ones.

Yes, I meant exactly that. And I believe the Bible supports this view. Let's begin by looking at the life of the Lord Jesus.

Our Lord is the eternal Son of God. While He did not cease to be God in His incarnation, He lived on earth as a perfect human being. He is therefore our great example. There is no doubt that He was very conscious of His Father's will, and that He fulfilled it completely. He declared, "I have come down from heaven not to do my own will but to do the will of him who sent me" (John 6:38). "The One who sent me is with me; . . . for I always do what pleases him" (John 8:29). "For I did not speak of my own accord, but the Father who sent me commanded me what to say and how to say it" (John 12:49).

An Old Testament scripture portion considered to be a prophetic prediction of the life of Christ states, "He [God] wakens me morning by morning, wakens my ear to listen like one being taught" (Isaiah 50:4). In view of these statements from both Testaments it is difficult to think of Jesus making even small decisions without God's guidance. Since you and I have been sent into the world as the representatives of Jesus (John 17:18), it is reasonable to believe that this step-by-step concern with God's will should also be characteristic of us.

Next, let's consider that wonderful Bible passage we call the Lord's prayer. It states, "Your will be done on earth as it is in heaven" (Matthew 6:10). These words indicate that God wants men and women on earth to follow His will as completely as they would if they were in His presence in glory. For people to be able to make the decisions God wills, God's active guidance would have to be available on a daily basis.

This conclusion finds confirmation in other passages of scripture. The apostle Paul's prayer in Colossians 1:9 has already been cited. Paul's desire was that Christians would be not simply aware of God's purposes but *filled* with the knowledge of His will. The same apostle told us in Ephesians 5:17 that, in order to make the most of every opportunity to serve the Lord, we must "understand what the Lord's will is."

Christians testify to God's concern about small things. The British army general Sir William Dobbie became famous as the "hero of Malta" during the dark early days of World War II, when as its commander he held that tiny Mediterranean island against incessant German bombardment. He wrote, "It is outstandingly true that God is willing and able to give help and wisdom in every problem, big and small, private and professional, and will demonstrate that this is so if we make a habit of taking all our problems to Him" (52-53).

A well-loved old preacher named George McCandless, who spent many nights at our home when I was a child, had faith that God would guide in even the smallest matters, and testified that this conviction had been confirmed by experience. "If you mislay a pencil while working at your desk," I heard him say, "it is quite in order to ask, 'Father, guide me in finding it,' and to expect Him to do so."

Finally, let me describe an incident involving one of my friends, a man committed to personal evangelism. Each day before leaving his home, he asked God to guide him in his witness. He then selected tracts that he thought he should use. One day he passed near a railroad yard, saw a Pullman car standing empty on a siding, entered it, and left several tracts. One was found by a railroad employee who had been praying to God for spiritual enlightenment. The message of the tract answered in a remarkably specific way the questions that were troubling him, and as a result he accepted Christ as his Savior. I was present a few years later when these two men met and were able for the first time to put the parts of the story together.

Most of us would agree that God had a hand in this incident. If so, we must also recognize that the delivery of the tract to the one who needed it was the result of a number of small choices made by my friend. His decision to distribute literature, the selection of the tracts, and the decision to place them in the Pullman car were all part of God's solution to the railroad employee's problem. Since my friend had prayed for guidance, the obvious conclusion is that he received it.

But what about really small decisions? Is God interested in what coat or shoes I choose to wear or what I have to eat?

According to the view of guidance presented in this book, the answer has to be yes.

This is too much! Am I to wait for a special sign from God before deciding between orange and tomato juice at breakfast tomorrow?

Of course not. God doesn't want you spending your time looking for signs.

Well then, how does He guide me in these things? And incidentally, if God is going to make all my decisions for me, what am I supposed to use my brains for?

Wait a minute! No one said that God wants you to spend time looking for signs, or that He is going to make any decisions, large or small, for you. We're talking about His guiding you in the decision process, which is another thing entirely. You are the one who makes each decision and God expects your brain to be fully involved. He doesn't want you to be a puppet, dancing on a string, but a mature, sensible Christian. The rest of this book is about *how* He guides.

One more question, Why does God care about my daily decisions? Why does He want to guide me?

According to the Bible, God has at least two purposes for His guidance. First, God wants to transform you into the likeness of Christ (Ephesians 4:13; 2 Corinthians 3:18). Second, He wants you to use your abilities for His glory as Jesus used His, so that those around you may recognize that Christ is real and the gospel is true (Acts 1:8; John 17:18-23). To put it bluntly, the purpose of divine guidance is not to help you do what you want, but what God wants. The other side of the coin, of course, is that what God wants is also best for you. True happiness can only come if you are doing His will.

Unfortunately, many believers have not grasped the truth of God's purposes for them. While they are thankful for God's salvation, they view the daily Christian life as a burden, a rather dismal tramp through the desert of this world. The goal of these Christians seems to be to get through each day with their faith reasonably intact, to "hang on" until they can be revived and encouraged by the next inspiring sermon, Bible study, or retreat experience.

To those who grasp the truth of God's guidance, on the other hand, life is not a bleak wilderness journey but an exhilarating climb toward higher ground, with the view getting better all the time. Each daily experience becomes a part of God's plan to fit them for their mission here on earth, and their role in the life to come. Like the apostle Paul, they see the final change from earth to heaven as simply the taking off of an earthly body and the assuming of a heavenly one (2 Corinthians 5:1).

There is an innate need within every human being to feel that his or her life is worthwhile, to find meaning of some sort in daily life. For you as a Christian, this need can be met as you realize that God is working in your life through His guidance to form you into the likeness of Jesus Christ. The more you allow Him to work in you, the quicker and more complete will be the molding process, and the more satisfying your companionship with Him. The importance of this molding is shown by the fact that God has sent His Holy Spirit into the lives of Christians to oversee the process.

QUESTIONS

1. What are the characteristics of the "traditional view" of guidance?

2. What are the characteristics of the second view of guidance described in this chapter?

3. What are the characteristics of the "middle ground" position proposed in this book?

4. What are some of the statements made by Jesus Himself which suggest that He received guidance from His Father during His life on earth?

5. What practical dilemma faces you if you adopt the view that God guides only in moral decisions?

6. In the story of the man who left literature in the Pullman car, what actions, which might have been considered unimportant in themselves, proved to have a significant impact on the result God wanted to bring about?

7. What is the difference between divine guidance and expecting God to make your decisions for you?

8. What factors cause some believers to think of the Christian life here on earth as a journey through a desert?

9. What scriptural truths encourage you to think of the Christian life as an exhilarating climb toward higher ground?

10. According to the Bible, what are two reasons why God chooses to guide you?

CHAPTER 4

The Holy Spirit—That Voice Behind You

This may be the most important chapter in this book. In a very real sense, understanding God's guidance means understanding what the Holy Spirit of God wants to do in your life. • When you received the Lord Jesus Christ as your Savior, the Holy Spirit came to live within you (John 14:16-17; Romans 8:9b). The responsibilities of the Holy Spirit are many. Some of them are: • The Holy Spirit seals you as His own, and makes your body His temple, or house (Ephesians 1:13; 1 Corinthians 6:19). • He links you together with other Christians in God's universal church (1 Corinthians 12:13). • He stands ready to help you understand the scriptures, reveal Christ to you, become your counselor, and guide you (John 16:7, 13-14). • He makes His own spiritual power available to you (Acts 1:8). • He fits you for your place of Christian service, giving you a special "gift" to be used for God (1 Corinthians 12:4-11). • He develops in you, if you allow Him, the actual characteristics of Christ: the attributes of love, joy, peace, patience, kindness, goodness, faithfulness, gentleness, and self-control (Galatians 5:22-23).

Not all of these workings of the Holy Spirit come about automatically or even at the same time. If you are to see God's plan come true in your life, the presence of the Holy Spirit must be not just a point of doctrine to be accepted, but a reality to be lived. And what a reality! God Himself has taken up residence in your body, for the Holy Spirit is God.

The book of Isaiah contains sections that describe the glorious future God has planned for His people Israel. In one of these the prophet described the role of divinely appointed teachers in these words, "Whether you turn to the right or to the left, your ears will hear a voice behind you, saying, 'This is the way; walk in it'" (Isaiah 30:21). In these New Testament times God's Holy Spirit is your teacher. While you cannot see Him, His eyes are on your life, and He stands ready in a gentle way to correct every false step. That "voice behind you" is an apt and graphic description of His function.

The Spirit's Role in Guidance

The first Bible reference to any truth is usually significant, often serving as a key to understanding that truth. The first reference in which the Holy Spirit is specifically linked to guidance is in Exodus 31:1-5. God had given to Moses on mount Sinai the pattern for a portable sanctuary, a center of worship for the tribes of Israel, called the "tabernacle." To construct this building and its intricately worked furnishings of gold, silver, bronze, and acacia wood, God chose a craftsman named Bezalel, and filled him with God's Spirit. As a result of this filling, Bezalel would "know how to carry out all the work of constructing the sanctuary" (Exodus 36:1). This scripture clearly connects the Holy Spirit with the active guidance of a human being, and suggests that the filling of the Spirit is required for following guidance effectively.

We read of the Spirit's guidance in a number of other Old

Testament passages, where it is recorded that He directed various prophets, kings, and others in spiritual and practical service for God. When we turn to the gospels and the book of Acts we find evidence that His guidance continued in New Testament times.

We have already discussed God's guidance in the life of Jesus. The channel for this guidance was the Holy Spirit. The public ministry of Jesus began only after the Holy Spirit descended on Him at His baptism (Luke 3:22). Immediately after that event, He was "led by the Spirit in the desert where . . . he was tempted by the devil" (Luke 4:1-2). Subsequently He returned "in the power of the Spirit" to Galilee (Luke 4:14). The placement of these statements at the beginning of the account of Jesus' service for God is a strong indication that the guidance of the Holy Spirit continued throughout His ministry.

The Holy Spirit also guided the lives of Jesus' followers. The witness of Christians began with the coming of the Holy Spirit on the day of Pentecost (Acts 2:1-4). Later on, it was the Holy Spirit who directed Philip to an Ethiopian in need of salvation (Acts 8:29), who led Peter to take the gospel to the gentile Cornelius (Acts 10:19-20), who sent Paul and Barnabas (Acts 13:2-4), and who guided the apostles on their missionary journeys (Acts 16:6-7; 21:4).

Notice that the Spirit's guidance in these cases was not limited to spiritual activities but included practical matters as well, and that small decisions as well as large ones were included. The guidance of Bezalel, for example, surely involved hundreds of decisions he made each day as he worked God's designs into wood and metal. In the case of Jesus, the Spirit's first guidance was to direct Him to the spot in the wilderness of Judea where the devil awaited Him. In the life of Paul, the Holy Spirit was concerned with the itinerary of the touring apostolic team, barring them from one destination while pointing them toward another.

On the basis of these scripture portions, the Holy Spirit appears to have the primary responsibility within the godhead for guiding human beings both in spiritual matters and in the more mundane decisions of daily life. When Paul wrote, "Those who are led by the Spirit of God are sons of God" (Romans 8:14), he was paying tribute to this ministry of the Spirit.

Being Filled with the Spirit

If you want to take best advantage of this guidance, the ideal condition is to be "filled" with the Spirit (Ephesians 5:18), as was Bezalel.

Bible teachers agree that the filling of the Spirit is an experience separate from conversion; it can come at the time of conversion or afterward. Most also agree that a Christian can have more than one filling; a person can be filled at one time and not filled at another. However, opinions differ as to whether the first time an individual is filled with the Spirit is necessarily a sudden, dynamic experience, or whether it may in some cases occur gradually as the Christian grows in spirituality. Entire volumes have been written about the Spirit-filled life. Here I will list only a few key points:

• All Christians are commanded to be filled with the Spirit; therefore being Spirit-filled is both desirable and possible.
• The Spirit entered your life at conversion; being Spirit-filled doesn't mean getting more of the Spirit, but letting Him have more of you.
• If you want to pack clothes in a trunk already full of rags, you must first empty it; you must let God take over and clean the "trash" out of your life if you want His Spirit to fill it.

• There is no scripture which states that the filling of the Spirit must be accompanied by miraculous signs. Those who teach that such signs must be in evidence if you are truly Spirit-filled base their case on inferences drawn from a few passages in the gospels and the book of Acts. (Miraculous signs will be discussed further in chapter 9.)

The scriptures present the state of being full of the Spirit as a normal Christian condition. If you allow God's Spirit to fill you each day, others will see the results in the form of spiritual fruit (the nine virtues of Galatians 5:22-23), which the Lord will produce in your life. In addition, you will experience, in a full and satisfying way, the Spirit's guidance.

Since God wants to fill you with His Spirit, you can trust Him to fill you if you commit your life to Him and seek the spiritual fulfillment He has for you. Total commitment is the important prerequisite.

How the Spirit Guides

Romans 12:1-2 shows that personal commitment will lead to knowing God's will. The steps are:

1. Make a definite prayerful decision to yield your body to Him. Put your future in His hands.

2. Don't let the world's way of life, its ambitions, and its attractions get a stranglehold on your life. "Renew" your mind each day by prayer and study of God's word.

3. God will then reveal His perfect will in your life.

Just as guidance is needed on a daily basis, so the commitment described in points 1 and 2 must be reaffirmed daily. When you have complied with these conditions, God can and will reveal His will to you through the Holy Spirit who indwells you.

It would be wrong to say that Christians who have not

yet made a full commitment of their lives to Christ do not receive guidance, because they do. But, it is likely that a child of God who is living partly or entirely for self may sometimes not recognize guidance when it comes, or if he does, may not be inclined to follow it.

Two homes can have identical furnaces. However, on a cold winter's day, one may be flooded with warm air; the other, where the thermostat is set lower, may be only a notch above the freezing point. In the same way, God's guidance is available to every Christian. The furnace is installed, so to speak, when you are saved; the extent to which it works is up to you. There is no energy shortage in God's economy. You can pay the "heating bill"—the cost of personal dedication—and experience the filling and guiding of God's Holy Spirit. Or you can cater to self and settle for a "low temperature" spiritual existence where the Holy Spirit's influence is barely evident in your life.

In the latter case your experience with guidance is likely to be meager. Christians in this condition often ignore God in their daily decisions, turn somewhat frantically to prayer when choices become difficult or trouble strikes, and go through life uncertain as to when, how, or even whether God has actually guided them.

But suppose you are a Christian who truly wants to live for God but has trouble doing so? Perhaps there are times when God's word and His purposes mean everything to you, and other times when the dam seems to break and things of this world and of your own desires roll over you in a flood, swamping your spiritual life entirely. Cheer up! No one said that living for God would be easy, only that it would be wonderful. Remember that there is a powerful spiritual enemy who is doing his best to discourage you and wreck your Christian life. If your goal is to serve Christ, you have taken the first big step.

Life's hardest battles are those you will face within yourself as you determine to learn, on a daily basis, how to let His Spirit rule in your life. Every Christian from the apostle Paul on has faced this problem (read chapter 7 of his letter to the Romans). It is solved through a spiritual learning process, carried on under the best and most patient of teachers. This learning aspect of the Christian life has been called "God's school," and the teacher is, of course, the Holy Spirit.

QUESTIONS

1. What do John 14:16-17 and Romans 8:9 tell you about the Holy Spirit's connection with the believer?

2. State in your own words what each of the following scripture passages indicates about the Holy Spirit.

Ephesians 1:13	John 16:7,13,14
1 Corinthians 12:4,11,13	Acts 1:8
1 Corinthians 6:19	Galatians 5:22

3. What can you conclude from Luke 4:1,14 about the way Jesus was guided during His earthly ministry?

4. What are some incidents recorded in the book of Acts that describe how the Holy Spirit guided the early Christians?

5. What does Romans 8:14 tell you about the activity of the Holy Spirit?

6. Summarize in your own words what Ephesians 5:18 says about being filled with the Spirit. Why do you think Paul contrasts being Spirit-filled with being drunk?

7. How can you be filled with the Spirit?

8. What are the three steps, found in Romans 12:1-2, to finding God's will? Why is it necessary for you to reaffirm frequently steps 1 and 2 ?

9. What are some ways in which you might conform to the pattern of this world, and how can you avoid this?

10. If we settle for less than full dedication to God in our daily lives what will be the probable effect on the guidance we receive from God?

CHAPTER 5

God's School

Industrial organizations often sponsor on-the-job training programs, in which the student/employee learns to do his job by actually working at it. "OJT," as it is abbreviated, has two purposes: first, the young worker gets the training he needs, and second, he accomplishes something useful while learning. Christians are guided in doing God's work during their stay on earth and, at the same time, grow into Christian maturity through the development of spiritual insight and judgment. • It was this process that Paul had in mind when he said: "Work out your salvation . . . for it is God who works in you to will and to act according to his good purpose" (Philippians 2:12-13). Since no human lifetime is long enough for us to learn all God wants us to know, we are enrolled in God's OJT for all of our time on earth. • What God wants to develop in you is a daily, harmonious collaboration in which every bit of your human capability to think, plan, and decide is used in a spirit of faith and dependence on Him. This collaboration may be a little like what happens when a father helps his son build a birdhouse. With his greatly superior knowledge and skill, the father could easily do all the work (just as God could make all our decisions for us if He wished). Instead, the wise dad guides the boy's hands so that the son, rather than the father, is doing the building. And, nail by nail, board by board, the child is learning adult skills.

There is a considerable difference in guidance when it is given with the aim of training in view, and when training is not the aim. If, for example, you were hired as a chauffeur, you would drive under your employer's direction. He would tell you where he wanted to go, possibly even what route to take, and how quickly or slowly to drive. He would probably give little thought to whether or not his guidance helped your ability as a driver. If, on the other hand, a friend were teaching you how to drive a car, the situation would be different. While the driving would, as before, be done under someone else's direction, the instructions you received would be designed not only to get the car to its destination, but also to help you learn to make the decisions and execute the maneuvers involved in driving. For example, to help you acquire the skill and judgment an experienced driver should have, the instructor might send you by a roundabout route through difficult traffic, rather than by a shorter, simpler way.

Similarly, God uses guidance to train you. As you learn your lessons, you can begin to see life's problems as God sees them, and to respond as Jesus would respond. True, the training process is not easy. It is a twenty-four hour-a-day program. It is a course that will challenge you to use every bit of your spiritual resources, your brains, your judgment, and your imagination. Yet it is one in which the instructor never loses patience when a student fails a test, and in which even the slowest pupil can succeed.

Looking at each day's experience as part of God's OJT can help you resolve conflicting ideas about guidance. If your daily decisions are elements in God's training program, you can dispense with the notion that God doesn't care what choices you make. You can also stop worrying about a single bad decision causing you to miss "God's best." While failures are never desirable or pleasant, faulty choices in a training environment become mistakes to learn from. In God's school, the fact that you err may be less important than whether or not you learn to do better. We will discuss the problem of wrong choices in more detail in chapter 13.

Textbook

The textbook used in God's school is the Bible, composed of sixty-six volumes written by some forty authors over a span of more than a thousand years. Two key New Testament passages assure us that the Bible is inspired by God, and that this inspiration occurred because the Holy Spirit directed the authors as they wrote God's messages (2 Timothy 3:16; 2 Peter 1:19-21). As we will see when we discuss the ways God guides, the Bible can be an important source of direct guidance for daily decisions.

Communication

If you were to join a French language class, you would probably find the instructor insisting that classroom conversation be in French to help you learn to use the language comfortably. God wants you to learn here on earth, which is His classroom, to communicate with Him. The means of communication is prayer.

Prayer can be thanking God for who He is and what He has done, asking Him to help in the problems of the day, or simply talking with Him. Most of us put the thoughts we want to express to God into words, even for silent prayer, though thoughts without words can be prayers too. Prayers can be addressed to God the Father in the name of Jesus, or to the Lord Jesus directly. Some also pray to the Holy Spirit; however, other Christians point out that we don't find direction to pray to the Spirit in scripture. In any case, the Bible states clearly that the Holy Spirit helps you to pray (Romans 8:26).

It is a good idea to begin each day by speaking to God, but you shouldn't let your prayer life stop there. You can pray anywhere and at any time. A Christian friend who travels a great deal by automobile tells me that he makes a consistent effort to use his driving time for prayer, and that this practice has made a major difference in his Christian life.

Prayer is more important to your life and mine than we may realize. When the Bible says, "Pray continually," this suggests that you should use every opportunity during the day to talk with God. This constant use of prayer will not only keep you from drifting into sin and selfishness, but will also allow the Lord to teach you of Himself in many small and subtle ways. Most important of all, from the point of view of our subject, consistent prayer will keep the channel of communication between you and God clear for the flow of His guidance into your life.

Training in Action

The idea that God wants you to "learn while doing" is not strange when you consider that it is precisely the approach taken in many purely human endeavors. Consider, for example, the relationship of a high school or college football coach and his quarterback. The job of the quarterback is directing the team. But the plays he calls on the field are designed to carry out the will of the coach. The coach is both guide and teacher, and the player is learning and directing at the same time.

How is the quarterback guided? Let us consider a case in which at least some plays are chosen by the quarterback and not signalled in from the bench. The quarterback is given a playbook, which he memorizes thoroughly. He learns the important rules which the coach has laid down for the team. He acquires, through personal contact and discussion with the coach, an understanding of good football and a clear idea of the "game plan" for each successive contest. Finally, during the game itself, he looks to the coach for active direction.

On the playing field, the quarterback faces a series of decisions. He calls the plays, making full use of his resources: his list of authorized plays, the coach's game plan, and certain special rules ("Don't throw a pass inside your own twenty-yard line without my OK!"). Most important, the quarterback applies to each game situation the kind of analysis that he knows his coach wants him to make. During the game, either the coach or the player may feel that additional guidance is needed. A substitute may run on to the field with a key play, or the quarterback in difficulty may look to the bench for a sign. In a critical situation, he may call a "timeout" and run to the sidelines for a personal conference with the coach.

You will note from this description that the relationship between the coach and the player is not as simple as it may appear. For example, it would be a mistake to say that the coach, simply because he stays on the sidelines, is not involved in the game, or that there is any part of the action in which he is not interested. The coach not only has a complete understanding of the activity on the field, but he also has very definite ideas as to what should be done. The quarterback's job is to carry out his coach's will by directing the team as nearly as possible in the way the coach himself would guide if he were calling the signals. To accomplish his coach's will, the quarterback uses his own will and skill at its disciplined best, with help from the bench supplied as necessary. The more nearly the coach and quarterback are in tune, the more smoothly and accurately this decision-making system works.

If you are not sports-oriented, the teaching profession may provide a better example of on-the-job training. A student teacher, with responsibility for a roomful of students, makes dozens of decisions per day under the watchful eye of a senior instructor and grows in skill and experience during the process. Like the quarterback, she has resources: her background of training, the course plan, classroom textbooks, school regulations. As each problem arises, she makes a quick mental check of the school rules and policies to see whether any of these apply. She calls on her intelligence, her technical knowledge and skill, and what she has learned from her own teachers. And she is expected to know when a problem should be referred to a higher authority.

As a member of God's OJT program, you start, as do the teacher and the quarterback, with a reference book (the Bible), knowledge of God's moral law, and experience with God's ways in the past. You also have (or should have) a desire to do your master's will. You are expected to make daily decisions using your intelligence, your judgment, and guidance supplied by the Lord.

Or course, these and all other pictures fall short of showing the full dimension of God's guidance. Since the Holy Spirit is within you, you aren't limited in your contact with your divine leader, so His guidance can be truly continuous. Moreover, God has more ways to direct you than any earthly leader has. The next chapter describes some of these methods.

QUESTIONS

1. What are the basic purposes of God's on-the-job training program?

2. Does Philippians 2:12-13 indicate that you must work your way to heaven? If not, what does the passage mean?

3. How does the illustration of the birdhouse help in understanding Philippians 2:12-13?

4. As a student in God's program, how should you view the unexpected problems and difficulties that crop up in your life?

5. How do the illustrations of the driver/trainee and the chauffeur help you understand God's ways of teaching?

6. What do 2 Timothy 3:16 and 2 Peter 1:19-20 tell you about the validity of the Bible, your textbook in God's course?

7. How does prayer fit into your learning process? What are some kinds of prayer you can use?

8. What does 1 Thessalonians 5:17 mean when it says "pray continually"? What are some benefits of continual prayer?

9. What times in your own daily schedule could be used for prayer?

10. How do the examples of the quarterback and the student teacher illustrate God's training program? In what ways do each of these illustrations fall short as a parallel to the Christian life?

CHAPTER 6

The Way God Guides

My father-in-law was an expert machinist, who maintained a basement workshop well-stocked with tools of many shapes and sizes: files, wrenches, screwdrivers, drills and many more. These were grouped in wall holders, and in drawers of his worktable. One of his skills, reflected in the fine results he achieved, was his ability to select exactly the right tool for each job. • In His dealings with us, God's Holy Spirit also uses a variety of tools, which are His ways of guidance. Like my father-in-law's tools, God's methods can be divided into categories, based on how He uses them. Some of these tools are:

Basic means of guidance
   1. Scriptures
   2. Human authority
   3. Past experience with God

Additional means
   4. Thought guidance
   5. Counsel of other Christians
   6. Circumstances
   7. Special messages

Means used to confirm other guidance
   8. Peace of mind

More often than not, the means of guidance in the first category serve as a framework or environment within which you will make your decisions, although occasionally God may use one of these resources as a direct and active way of influencing your decisions.

Of the four methods in the second category, thought guidance is the one that, in my experience, God employs most often. The counsel of wise and mature Christians is invaluable in certain decisions. God seems to use circumstances more frequently to support other means of guidance than as a primary means. Special messages are rare indeed, and should not be expected in the normal course of events.

The guidance method in the final category, peace of mind, often helps to resolve lingering doubts about decisions already made.

It is true that the Bible nowhere gives us a specific list like the one above. However, for these eight there is scriptural support, and all have been confirmed through the experiences of Christians.

One danger in writing such a list is that it may start you wondering why God hasn't used all of the tools listed in your own life. The British humorist J. K. Jerome described how he read through a medical book and became convinced that he had the symptoms of nearly all the major diseases. When you read or hear about how God has guided others, especially the more dramatic cases, it is only natural to begin looking for the same sort of divine direction in your own life. The truth is that God uses, for each person individually, the kind of guidance that suits his need, his faith, and his personality. If there is any general rule, it is that God seems to use simple means much more often than spectacular ones.

Let's look at the listed means of guidance in more detail.

1. Scriptures. God's word is a lamp for our feet and a light for our path (Psalm 119:105). God's word is a most important source of guidance, for it contains the principles of Christian living. The Bible defines the righteous life that God wants you to live. From the scriptures you learn that you should pray continually, love other believers and meet regularly with them, be a good witness for Christ, treat everyone fairly without discrimination, and help those in need.

The verse, "Do not lie to each other" (Colossians 3:9), for example, has been effective in keeping some of us from "bending" the truth to our own advantage. The Bible command, "Do not let the sun go down while you are still angry" (Ephesians 4:26), followed literally can provide effective guidance for settling family differences on the same day they arise.

Even where a specific scriptural command does not exist, you will often find clear-cut principles in the Bible which apply. Daily Bible reading is important to keep you in tune with God's revelation and to help you keep your life clean (Psalm 119:9). The influence of God's word can help you in making right choices even in cases where you do not have a specific verse on which to hang your decision.

If you are thinking about doing something contrary to the directions or principles found in the Bible, there is no use in praying for special guidance. You already have it.

2. Human authority. All through life you are subject to existing authorities. As young people you are under parents and teachers. Later on, there are employers, superiors in military service, and representatives of local, state, and national governments whose laws and regulations you must obey.

The Bible says that it is your duty as a Christian to obey the legitimate authorities in your life (Romans 13:1). The only exception is the case in which someone in authority requires you to do something contrary to a direct command of God.

Any rule, for example, which forbids you to acknowledge God or worship Him should be disobeyed (Acts 5:28-29).

Since God asks you to obey human authorities, you are justified in looking on their dictates as part of His guidance. As a matter of fact, Paul spoke of governmental rulers as God's servants or ministers to the Christian (Romans 13:4). Just as God used the decree of Caesar Augustus to bring Joseph and Mary to Bethlehem in time to fulfill the prophecies about Jesus' birth, so He can use parents, teachers, policemen, and employers in guiding you.

A few years ago, I taught a Bible class after hours in a local high school (this was before such activity on public school grounds was forbidden). One of the most enthusiastic members was a girl whose parents were antagonistic to the gospel. In her senior year they decided she was becoming too involved with Christian activities and told her she must drop them. They did not order her to renounce her faith in Jesus Christ—that, of course, she could not have done—but only to give up Bible class and similar functions. Though it was difficult for her she realized that, as a young person still under her parents' authority, she should obey. The rules they laid down she viewed correctly as God's guidance for her. She went on to graduate with honors, still a happy Christian, and one who hoped through her love and obedience to win her parents to Christ.

3. Past experience with God. God can also use your knowledge of His past dealings to guide you. A well-known psalm tells us that by observing God's working in human lives we can understand His lovingkindness (Psalm 107:43). Jesus suggested that by serving Him (taking His yoke), we will learn of Him (Matthew 11:29). When an instructor shows a student how to do something, he expects that the student will begin to practice the new technique, and to master it. In the same way, God expects you to learn from your association with Him. Even experience that has involved failure on your part can be valuable. Recall that the apostle Peter was, as a result of his own failure, able to strengthen others (Luke 22:32).

My Christian faith was badly shaken, as a student, by the apparent conflict between science and the Bible. The Holy Spirit guided me gently through this crisis but, because of my spiritual weakness, it took years before my faith in the scriptures was reestablished. During my subsequent career in the scientific field, I have occasionally been faced with challenges against the Bible, leveled by misguided people in the name of science. I did not, at those times, feel the need to go through my earlier crisis of faith again. The guidance once given was sufficient. I have also found, as Peter did, that my past failure can be made useful. Because of my experience, I am often able to understand in a special way other young people who are troubled by the relationship of science to the scriptures, and to help them to a better understanding.

In the same way God wants you to regard the experiences of life as lessons from Him. As you learn what they have to teach, you will grow in strength and maturity in the Christian faith.

4. Thought guidance. God uses this means of guidance every day in the lives of Christians. By this means God guides our smallest decisions, and it is no less useful in major matters. Because it is less clearly understood than some other types of guidance, I will consider it in some detail.

We have already identified God's Holy Spirit as the main agent of divine guidance. Since He indwells you, His influence is applied internally, that is, through your mental processes. When you commit your way to God, His Spirit influences your thinking in quiet, natural ways to guide you to His will. He can help you see through the complexities of a problem, and give you the perspective you need for a solution.

Thought guidance is implied in some of the verses we have previously looked at concerning the Holy Spirit. Other scriptures are even more specific. Paul described a person who is committed to Christ as having a "mind controlled by the Spirit" (Romans 8:6), and indicated his own desire to "take captive every thought to make it obedient to Christ" (1 Corinthians 10:5).

Since thought guidance is the result of communication between the Spirit of God and the mind and spirit of the believer, it is not surprising that some of the clearest testimonies about this kind of guidance come from Christians who have lived especially close to the Lord.

One such person was Brother Lawrence. He was a member of a French monastery in the seventeenth century, and his experiences, recorded by a contemporary, have been published in a little book, *The Practice of the Presence of God*. Lawrence's conviction was that "we ought to act very simply with God, speaking familiarly with Him, and asking Him for help in situations as they arise. God would not fail to give it as he [Lawrence] had often experienced."

Brother Lawrence was convinced that God guided his thought processes during the daily tasks he was required to perform. We read that when he was required to act as a purchasing agent for his monastery, a role for which he felt totally unfitted, "he did not however trouble himself about this . . . he told God that it was His business, after which he found that everything worked out and worked out well." In another similar situation, "it was not he [Lawrence] who managed it and it turned out very well" (23).

Another believer who lived in close communion with God was George Washington Carver, well known for his scientific research, which resulted in the development of many useful products from peanuts and sweet potatoes. He said,

"I never grope for methods. The method is revealed the moment I am inspired to create something new. . . . I gather specimens and listen to what God has to say to me. After my morning's talk with God I go into my laboratory and begin to carry out His wishes for the day. It is not we little men that do the work, but our blessed Creator working through us."

Because thought guidance is gentle and unobtrusive, it is easy to ignore. God will not force it on you. It was prominent in the lives of Brother Lawrence and George Washington Carver because both were men of prayer who were fully yielded to God, and who believed firmly in God's moment-by-moment guidance.

5. Counsel of other Christians. Proverbs 20:18 says, "Make plans by seeking advice." The New Testament tells us to encourage each other and spur one another to do good (Hebrews 10:24-25). Receiving advice from other Christians does not absolve you from making your own decisions, but it can help in pointing the way to the best solution.

The choice of a counselor is, of course, very important. It is usually easy to find people willing to tell you what you should do in any situation—sometimes even before you ask for advice! All available counsel may not be spiritual, even when it comes from Christians. The counselor should be someone who is truly spiritual (some believers, even though they may have had years of Christian experience, are spiritually dormant), and who has the quality of wisdom that sees both sides of a question. It is also helpful if your adviser knows something about the particular type of problem you are facing. If the one counseling you is a great deal older than you are, it is important that he or she be able to see things from a younger person's point of view. Ask the Lord to help you pick the right person as your counselor.

There have been several Christians who have influenced

my life profoundly through wise counsel. They were of different personalities, but all were spiritual, possessed sound judgment, and were willing to listen and to help. The important fact is that the Lord brought me in touch with each when I needed him.

6. Circumstances. Guidance through circumstances is what many Christians think of first when the subject of God's direction in daily life comes up. It is easy to magnify this type of guidance out of all proportion to its real value.

What is circumstantial guidance? It is simply God's use of events in your daily life to point you in the direction you should go. We know from the scriptures that "in all things God works for the good of those who love him, who have been called according to his purpose" (Romans 8:28). If you meet these requirements—that is, if you are motivated by love of God and are willing to recognize His purpose in your life—you can be confident that God will arrange the circumstances of your life for your good.

Circumstances can affect the direction of your life in at least three ways. Sometimes circumstances will force you into one course of action or another and it is important that you accept the results as God's will for you. When the young Joseph, in the book of Genesis, left home to visit his brothers, he was caught up in events beyond his control, and found himself a slave in Egypt, hundreds of miles away. Instead of giving way to despair, he recognized what had happened as part of God's plan. "It was not you who sent me here, but God," he told his brothers later (Genesis 45:8). Because of Joseph's faith, he was put in a position to save thousands of people, including his own family, from starvation during the years of famine.

A second form of circumstantial direction occurs when God uses events as indicators to help you understand His will in a particular situation. When the apostle Paul wrote the Corinthians that he would stay in Ephesus because "a great door" had been opened to him there (1 Corinthians 16:9), we gather that the unexpected circumstance of improved opportunities to spread the gospel was a factor in convincing him that God wanted him to change his plans. You too may find, when you have a choice to make between two courses of action, that circumstances may "work out" in the direction of one choice or the other. The "open door" may be an indication that God is guiding you toward that choice. By removing an obstacle, God can confirm your decision, and increase your assurance that you have decided correctly. By refusing to remove an obstacle, God can signal you to reconsider a choice.

Sometimes God's will must be done in spite of circumstances, and this is the case in which overemphasis on circumstantial guidance can be dangerous. If the great missionary explorer David Livingstone, for example, had taken each of the hurdles in his path as a sign from God to turn back, the great missionfield of Africa would probably not have been opened to the gospel during his lifetime. As it was, he regarded these obstacles as challenges and overcame them.

I will discuss later how the various types of guidance work together. A good initial rule to remember is that before being accepted as valid, circumstantial guidance should be supported and confirmed by some other means of divine direction.

7. Special messages. This type of divine direction is more often talked about than experienced. Stories of Christians who have received special messages of one sort or another from God are remembered and repeated because they are spectacular, but this method seems to be used less often than those previously discussed.

Paul's "Macedonian message" is an example of this type

of guidance. The apostle and his group had already been given guidance (of a sort not specified), which changed their proposed route through Bithynia to one farther west. When they reached Troas, Paul saw in a night vision a man from the Greek land lying to the west across the Aegean sea, who asked for help (Acts 16:9). God used this special message to send the group into a new missionary territory. Later in life Paul was given other special messages from God (for example, during his journeys to Jerusalem and Rome in Acts 21:4; 27:23).

Christians who are discouraged, or facing difficult problems, have sometimes been helped through a special verse of scripture or a line from a hymn, which has seemed to contain just the guidance needed for the problem in hand. Such messages are almost always unexpected; they are usually so clear and to the point that the Christian receiving them has no doubt what is meant. They seem to be given under circumstances where other means of guidance are unsuitable for some reason or in cases where the Christian needs special reassurance.

The problem with special-message guidance comes not so much when you *have* received it but when you would *like* to. Then you will be tempted to riffle through the pages of your Bible or scrutinize the words on the devotional calendar, trying to coax a message from God. Sad to say, coaxing doesn't work. God will send you a special message only if He decides you need one.

8. Peace of mind. "You will keep in perfect peace him whose mind is steadfast" (Isaiah 26:3). Paul stated that if you bring your problems to God with prayer and thanksgiving, you may expect the peace of God, which is beyond understanding, to keep your heart and mind (Philippians 4:7). These promises can be applied to divine guidance. If you yield to God's will, and commit the resultant decisions to Him, He will give peace of mind.

You may notice this state of peace particularly in cases where there was no strong guidance one way or the other, and you are not certain your decision was right. In such instances, when you have settled on a "best choice," you will often find that the Lord will confirm your decision by sending His own peace to your troubled mind.

In most cases, you will experience this peace of God only after a decision is made. However, the experience can also come during the decision-making process itself. Peace then takes the form of a God-given conviction as to what your choice should be. Whether before or after, this divine peace of mind in connection with your decisions is one of God's most wonderful gifts.

The value of peace of mind in God's guidance became especially evident to me a few years ago when I was faced with the problem of whether or not to make a major change in my professional career. It was a difficult decision, with good and bad points on each side, and my wife and I prayed over and struggled with the problem for weeks. Once the choice was made, God gave us both peace, even though the change seemed at first to create more problems than it solved. It was not until several years had passed that the wisdom of our choice became apparent in practical ways. During the interim, the Lord gave us, on a daily basis, confidence that we had made the right decision.

Some Christians are inclined to discount thought guidance and the guidance of peace of mind because these methods can not be supported by outward evidence. God's means of guidance, they maintain, should be objective —apparent to our five senses. The fact is that some significant truths of the Christian faith can not be confirmed by our senses. We know that we are saved, we understand that the Spirit indwells us, and we are certain of a home in heaven, not because we have sensory evidence of these truths, but because we have within us the testimony of the Holy Spirit that they are true. The working of divine guidance is similarly a matter for faith.

QUESTIONS

1. What are some possible reasons why God uses a number of different methods of guidance rather than just one or two?

2. What are some specific guidelines found in scripture that should regulate your conduct? What are some scriptural principles that provide more general guidance?

3. Who are the secular authorities in your life and why does God ask you to obey them?

4. What exception is given in scripture to the principle that you should obey the secular authorities over you? In what circumstance today might Christians be justified in disobeying their government?

5. What lessons concerning the guidance of past experience can be learned from Psalm 107:43; Matthew 11:29; Luke 22:32?

6. What two types of guidance are suggested in Psalm 32:8-9? Which one of these defines what this chapter calls "thought guidance"? In what sorts of situations might the Lord use this type of guidance in your own life?

7. What are some circumstances in which the counsel of other

Christians could be an important means of guidance? What characteristics should you look for in a counselor?

8. How does this chapter define circumstantial guidance? In what three ways do circumstances affect your life? What problems are likely to be encountered if you depend on circumstantial guidance alone?

9. God seems to use "special messages" as a means of guidance only rarely. Why is it unwise to expect that God will provide you with this type of guidance?

10. Under what circumstances are you likely to receive the guidance of "peace of mind"? How can you recognize this type of guidance when it occurs?

CHAPTER 7

Practical Applications

An Old Testament passage that speaks to our subject is Proverbs 3:1-6: "My son, do not forget my teaching, but keep my commandments in your heart, for they will prolong your life many years and bring you prosperity. Let love and faithfulness never leave you; bind them around your neck, write them on the tablet of your heart. Then you will win favor and a good name in the sight of God and man. Trust in the Lord with all your heart, and lean not on your own understanding; in all your ways acknowledge him and he will make your paths straight." • In the King James version, the latter part of verse 6 reads, "He will direct thy paths," a fact that resulted in the display of this text on many walls as a "guidance motto." However, since the Hebrew verb *yashar* used here can also be rendered "make straight (or smooth)," some scholars conclude that this passage does not refer to divine guidance at all. This conclusion is unfortunate, for "He will direct your paths" is still a valid translation. Even if the verse is rendered, "He will make your paths straight," divine guidance is implied. In any case, the passage as a whole is concerned with how to live a God-honoring life and hence is important to our study of guidance.

Let's see what the passage teaches:

First, keep God's word in your heart. You can do this by reading your Bible daily, and meditating or "mulling over" in your mind the truths you find there. It is also a good idea to memorize passages that are especially meaningful to you. Then you can repeat them to yourself at times when your Bible is not available.

Second, think often about God's love and faithfulness to you. Ask God to give you opportunities to demonstrate these Christ-like qualities in your relationships with others, and look for such opportunities.

Third, trust Him fully, and don't depend on your own wisdom. Practice the art of believing God's promises. Believe that He is faithful and rest in the assurance that His wisdom is available to help you in every problem.

Fourth, acknowledge Him. Begin by acknowledging to yourself His presence with you, and His desire to guide you. Recognize His interest in each choice you make in the course of a day. As you draw close to Him, God's presence will become increasingly real, and it will become easy to acknowledge Him before others as your Lord and Savior.

Fifth, expect Him to make your paths straight (or direct your paths). Commit each daily decision to Him. Then make these decisions promptly, firmly and confidently, believing that He is guiding you, and that the results will be glorifying to Him.

Notice that the effect of each element in this exhortation is to focus your attention on God. Once this focus is achieved, His guidance in your life through the various methods we have discussed will be recognized easily and naturally.

The human eye is so constructed that a sailor, standing night-lookout-watches at sea, can see a dim object more clearly by focusing on a point a little to one side of the object than by staring directly at it. Your spiritual vision is designed so that you can see God's will for you, not by concentrating on it, but by looking at Him. If you "acknowledge him" (verse 6) He will direct your paths. If He is the most important factor in your life, understanding His will is both easy and natural.

God's guidance includes small, medium-sized, and large decisions, decisions in the routine of daily life, and those in times of crisis. Let's see how God wants us to approach these choices.

Guidance in Little Things

All of us know of instances where insignificant acts have had lasting results. Someone throws a stone at a tin can, hits another person by mistake, and is involved in an expensive lawsuit. Someone else passes up a helping of salad at a cafeteria, and avoids food poisoning. There are many small decisions that can be important in ways we may never discover. How does God influence us in these seemingly insignificant decisions?

We have already talked about the importance of starting each day with a positive commitment of your body and life to God's service. (If you are as forgetful as I am, you may have to renew this commitment during the day.) It is also very desirable to read the Bible as early each day as possible, so that the Holy Spirit can use the scriptures to influence your daily decisions. Your morning "quiet time" provides a good opportunity for both scripture reading and daily personal commitment.

Once you have started the day in this way, you can view every subsequent event, no matter how small, as a part of God's plan for your life. As you are faced with decisions during the day, you can confidently expect God's Holy Spirit to direct you. Minor problems—those concerning what to eat, what to wear, whether to stop for gasoline now or later—you decide by simple logic, and usually without stopping to pray about them individually. This does not mean you are not being guided in these small decisions. You have God's promise to "make your paths straight." By influencing your thinking, the Holy Spirit within you helps you to reach each decision and preserves you from error.

Once in a while, as you look back over the events of a day, you may be able to distinguish God's hand in some of these apparently unimportant matters. Perhaps the dress or necktie you wore provided a conversational opening that permitted you to witness to someone, or a "chance" stop at a drugstore gave you some information valuable in your business. Incidents such as these should encourage you to trust God that all of your decisions have been similarly guided.

If you have time to spare before making even a small decision, it's a good idea to pray. The verse "pray continually" implies exactly that (1 Thessalonians 5:17). These prayers can be very simple: "Father, help me find my keys!" "Lord, please help me make this choice correctly." Having prayed, proceed ahead to solve the problem in faith that God has heard you, and that His eye, which is on the sparrow, is also on your pencil, and your workbench, and your school examination paper.

If a scriptural principle, or a rule or law of legitimate human authority, is involved in any problem, even a minor one, you must take this into account. The decision here is usually a straightforward one: you simply do what the Bible or the law says is right. Suppose, for example, you are confronted with a temptation to falsify an expense account or cheat on an examination. Following the plain guidance of scripture, and of the school or company rules, you refuse. No other guidance is required, and no other course of action can be justified.

If you are not certain whether a scriptural principle is involved or not, and an immediate decision is required, play it safe. Make the choice you are sure is all right, rather than one that is questionable. Later you may be able to clear up the problem using prayer, Bible study, and possibly the counsel of other Christians, so that you will be sure of your ground if the question arises again.

Help for Medium-Sized Problems

Suppose you have been invited to visit a friend in another city. You would like to accept. How should you decide whether or not to go?

You begin, of course, with the important step of telling the Lord that you want His will to be done. You pray about the problem in detail, considering each of the pros and cons. As a result of this process, you may feel somewhat certain that you should go. There are, however, some difficulties: money for the trip, arranging time off from work or school, someone to take your Sunday school class responsibility while you are away, parental permission if you are a young person living at home. Back to the prayer mat you go. You pray about each of these hindrances individually, and one by one they are removed. An income tax refund provides the funds, your boss is understanding about the time off, and there is a volunteer substitute for your class. You conclude that God is guiding you and confirming your decision.

If the funds are not available, or you just can't find someone to teach that important Sunday school class, you should review your initial decision. Perhaps the Lord is telling you that you shouldn't go after all. If so, you may receive, after prayer, some sort of confirmation in that direction.

In this example, the Lord used thought guidance supported by circumstances. Note that you can't assume every circumstance that "works out" is the Lord's will, and that every setback means that you have made a wrong choice. Circumstantial guidance must be considered with prayer. It may be used to confirm a decision rather than to help you make it. However, it can be a powerful tool to change you from one choice to another when you are headed in the wrong direction.

Making Big Decisions

Let's look at a major decision. You will face many such decisions in your Christian life, each of which will merit very serious thought and prayer. Should you make a major investment in a new car? Should you change to another job? Should you take responsibility for a Sunday school class? The characteristics of each of these problems are that the choice made could substantially affect your life for either a short- or long-range period.

As in the previous examples, your starting point here is your willingness to do whatever the Lord wants. And, as before, God's most frequent way of leading us forward from that point is to help us think the problems through. You should expect that He will make clear to you good reasons for doing one thing rather than another. If these reasons are still valid after you have earnestly prayed and reaffirmed to Him your desire to do His will alone, you can consider that you have God's blessing on your course of action, and you go ahead. To continue to wait, in a clear case such as this, until you have a special feeling of being led to make the decision, or until you receive some positive sign, would make the matter of guidance much more complicated and mystical than God intended, and may actually be spiritual laziness.

However, if there really are major uncertainties as to the right course still remaining, you may properly feel that these should be cleared up before you go ahead. If your prayers for guidance are not answered, it may be that you are not praying in a practical way. Instead of broadly stated prayers asking God to give you the answer to a big problem, you may need specific prayers about *parts* of the problem.

Elements of the Problem

Suppose, for example, you are trying to decide whether or not to quit your job and take another. Pray about the whole problem, certainly. But analyze it as well. Break it down into phases and pray about each of them in turn. Decide what you need to know to clarify each phase, and ask God for help in acquiring each of these pieces of information.

Consider first of all, the probable effect of this job change on your Christian service. Will your freedom to serve the Lord be increased or diminished? In today's high pressure world, this aspect of employment is especially important.

Is the problem of transportation to the new job a restraining factor? Pray that if it is the Lord's will for you to take the job, He will help you to obtain some positive information on car pools. Then check into car-pool possibilities. If you are given the name of a person who might share the driving with you, pray specifically that God will give you a clear indication, through a phone call to that person, as to whether or not a car pool can be formed. Look to God to open and close the door to this possibility.

If there is a salary problem, analyze it, and pray in a definite way for the specific pieces of the puzzle to fit together. Remember that the Old Testament stalwart Nehemiah, in praying about fulfilling his dream to rebuild Jerusalem, broke the problem down to the most specific of requests: "Grant [me] favor in the presence of this man [the king]" (Nehemiah 1:11).

While you are engaged in this analysis-and-prayer operation, keep current a pro and con list. As reasons *for* taking the new job emerge, record them; if new difficulties arise, set them down as well. Updating this list will tell you how you are progressing. It will also suggest new things to pray about.

Throughout this process it is important to maintain a "yielded" attitude toward the decision. Ask yourself periodically, "Am I willing to accept *either* solution to this question if I am convinced this solution is what God wants for me?" If your answer is yes, your prayers definite and pointed, your approach patient but confident in faith, you are on the right wavelength for God's solution.

If your experience with major decisions is similar to mine, you won't find this process easy. For one thing it will be a real exercise for some of your lesser-used muscles of prayer and faith. But as you pray about each part of the problem, you will begin to see bits of the dilemma clarifying. Some of the things that seemed to block the way may either dissolve or become more firm. Certain favorable aspects may develop unexpected weak points; others may, under scrutiny, become more favorable.

When Answers Don't Come

It is sometimes the case that the time for the decision arrives before all the questions have been answered, or all the difficulties removed. This is the time when faith is really put to the test. "Why," you ask, "doesn't God give me just a little more certainty about this thing?"

There may be many reasons why guidance is not as prompt or as clear as you would like. Perhaps you are not really willing to accept God's answer. Or maybe you need the extra practice in exercising faith. Still other factors may be involved. The prophet Daniel had his answer to prayer delayed by the forces of evil for three weeks (Daniel 10:2,12,13), even though God had responded promptly. This suggests that the power of Satan is sometimes sufficient to delay God's answers to us, for a deadly spiritual warfare that we know little about is going on all around us. Whatever the reason, God wants us to trust Him, and to proceed in faith.

It is dangerous to prescribe definite rules as to what you should do in specific cases (as we've said before, God guides each of us differently), but one or two general guidelines may help. If your important decision is a yes-or-no one, where the "yes" involves making a change (buying the car, taking the job, proposing to the girl) and the "no" means essentially leaving matters as they are now, then you should expect to be reasonably confident before taking the "yes" action. If you are not sure which choice to make, it is often better to say no, to leave things as they are, until you do get some assurance, rather than to plunge ahead into what might be a positive error. A lack of assurance in this case may be God answering in the negative.

Suppose, on the other hand, you have what might be called a this-or-that decision facing you, one in which you are faced with a basically even choice between two positive courses of action. For example, you may know that you have to take a summer job—the question is, which one of two available jobs should you take? Usually, in this sort of problem there is a deadline, a time by which one choice or the other must be made. In most cases you will find, if you have truly committed the problem to the Lord, that one choice will emerge as the right one before the decision must be made.

What should you do when decision time arrives and God's guidance is still not as definite as you would like, or when (as has happened to me on a few occasions) God appears to have withheld His guidance entirely? You should, without panic, proceed to make the choice that seems best on the basis of the evidence you have, trusting that through thought guidance God will make your final decision a right one.

Sometimes the counsel of another Christian can help. Since the Lord has instructed us to "carry each other's burdens" (Galatians 6:2), you should feel free to ask for advice. Again, there are a few general guidelines to keep in mind. First, don't ask someone else to decide *for* you. This is not fair to your adviser, and you will lose the lesson God has for you in solving the problem. Second, pick your guide with care. In chapter 6 we talked about the qualities to look for in a counselor. Third, think and pray over advice before acting on it. Give God a chance to show you any flaws in the counsel you have received.

Once you have made a right decision, you should expect to feel reasonably at peace about it. This is the guidance of peace of mind, most important to the Christian, and a safeguard we sometimes overlook. If, after a decision is made, your state of mind is troubled, it may be a clue that you should review your choice again.

Sometimes the reason for God's apparent lack of guidance will become clear to you afterward. A true story might illustrate this point. A Christian girl had to make a very important this-or-that decision—the choice of a university. At her request, her parents prayed with her for several weeks before decision time. On the last night they sat up until 2:00 a.m. trying to decide which of two possible schools was the Lord's choice. While each school had its good and bad points, the advantages and disadvantages were very evenly balanced, and there was a disconcerting lack of specific guidance in either direction. Finally, realizing a decision had to be made, they agreed on what seemed the best choice, filled out the form to be mailed and went to bed, trusting God to make it right. The next day, each of the three was individually troubled about the decision; however, each suppressed these feelings, believing that the other two were satisfied with the decision made. When the girl, with many misgivings, prepared to mail the papers, she suddenly found that she had misread the deadline date, and that there were two more weeks in which to make the final decision! When she and her parents met again to pray, the lack of peace of mind in the initial decision made was a major factor in helping the girl to decide confidently on the other school. In retrospect, this family believes God allowed them to reach the wrong decision first as a means of making clearer what the right one was.

Guidance in Emergencies

Just as God guides in everyday life, and in making specific decisions, so we can count on Him when crises arise. The Bible is full of promises that God will be near His own when trouble comes. We have many examples of God guiding His people in difficult times. Gideon, David, and Paul were all given specific direction by God in emergency situations. God's guidance in emergencies sometimes comes in unexpected ways, especially when there is a need for immediate direction and there is no time for other kinds of guidance to operate. Special messages, thought guidance (sometimes in the form of a strong, sudden conviction), or direction through a sudden change in circumstances, may be used by God to guide in time of crisis.

Perhaps the best way to explain guidance in emergencies is by describing one of the few occasions in my own life when I received this kind of guidance from God.

While driving on a highway, I came over the top of a hill, received the full glare of the rising sun in my eyes, and was momentarily blinded. Before my eyes cleared so that I could see the road ahead, I received a sudden overpoweringly strong directive (I can think of no better term) to jerk my steering wheel sharply to the right toward the highway's edge. I did so, and an oncoming car hurtled by me, missing a head-on collision by inches. I believe God used this method of guidance because it was the best way to meet the problem.

In other instances, when this urgency did not exist, God has not given me this type of guidance. If you have not been the subject of crisis guidance, don't worry about it. Its absence probably means only that you haven't needed it.

Putting It All Together

Before going on to a discussion of God's will in special situations, let's take another look at the passage in Proverbs, with which I began this chapter. It is worth looking at twice.

God's promise that He will make our paths straight if we acknowledge Him in all our ways is really a call to a life of faith. The New Testament confirms this call. In Paul's letter to the Colossians we read, "So then, just as you received Christ Jesus as Lord, continue to live in him" (Colossians 2:6).

How did you first receive Christ? By grace, through faith, and without works. How are you to to "live in Him" each day as a Christian? In the same way: by grace, through faith, and without works!

When you became a Christian, you realized that your own efforts could not save you. Salvation came when you stopped *trying* to be good, and simply trusted God's love and His promise to save you because of what Jesus did on Calvary's cross. God wants you and me to live by faith in just the same way: to stop struggling against life's problems, to relax and let Him lead.

This process, expressed in practical, daily living, is the real keynote of this chapter. God guarantees that living by faith will work for you if you are willing to put Him first in your life. Think for a moment what His promise of daily, down-to-the-smallest-item guidance means. It assures you that everything—*everything*—that happens to you in the course of the day has been reviewed in advance by God, and chosen by Him to be a part of your experience. And, as Romans 8:28 proclaims, it is for your good. God's promise also gives you a simple and foolproof way to approach every daily decision. You may find yourself expressing this approach in a little silent prayer, sent up to God hundreds of times during the day, as various situations arise: "Lord, what do *You* want me to do in this matter? Guide my decision, Lord."

This approach is really all it takes. When you and I have learned to commit each problem to God, step out boldly in faith to make whatever decision the situation requires, and finally drop the results into God's hands with a prayer of thanks without looking back afterward to worry uselessly about the results, we will begin to understand what the ancient prophet Habakkuk meant when he wrote long ago: "The righteous will live by his faith" (Habakkuk 2:4).

It is worth emphasizing that living by faith means living confidently. The picture of a Christian as a confused individual, waiting for some sign from God as to what decision to make, is false and should have no place in your thinking. You should approach your decisions with the common sense God has given you. Weigh the alternatives, pray about them, and remain sensitive to the various kinds of guidance God may elect to use. Then when the time for action comes, step out in faith and make firm decisions. God will be with you as He has promised and will honor your trust.

QUESTIONS

1. What are the five steps to a well-guided life, according to Proverbs 3:1-6?

2. In order to be guided in "little things," how should you prepare yourself at the beginning of each day? How should you make these decisions?

3. How should you handle small decisions in which a scriptural principle, or a rule established by a legitimate authority, is involved? What if you are not sure whether or not scriptural principles apply?

4. How does this chapter define a "medium-sized" decision, and a "big" decision? What initial step should be taken in approaching these types of decisions? Why is this first step important?

5. Why should you pray about specific details or parts of a problem, rather than simply asking God to guide your final choice? What sort of answers to these detailed prayers should you expect?

6. What is a pro and con list? How can making such a list help you in praying for guidance?

7. What is the difference between a yes-or-no decision and a this-or-that decision? What differences are you likely to find in the guidance God gives you in these two cases?

8. What can you do when an important decision needs to be made, and guidance does not seem to come?

9. Why might God's guidance in emergencies differ from His guidance in other situations? Why is it sometimes more spectacular?

10. How might the truth of Colossians 2:6 help you in following God's guidance?

God's Will and Your Christian Service

Near the end of His life on earth, Jesus stated that He was going to send His followers into the world as God had sent Him (John 17:18). Christians today have the responsibility to live as God's chosen servants on earth, as Jesus did. • The mission of every Christian includes at least the following parts: • 1. To represent God to other people—to be God's witness. • 2. To represent yourself and others before God—to be God's priest. • 3. To function as a member of God's family—to be a true brother or sister in Christ. • His guidance is necessary in fulfilling each part of this mission.

Guidance in Being a Witness

One of the titles given the Lord Jesus Christ is "the faithful witness" (Revelation 1:5). After His resurrection, Jesus told His followers that they also were to be witnesses (Acts 1:8), and all Christians today are witnesses for God. It is important that a witness be "faithful"; that is, consistent and in accordance with God's guidance.

If God's purpose were only to disseminate information about the gospel to as many people as possible as soon as possible, your service and mine as witnesses would not be needed. The program could be accomplished by "saturation" advertising, using billboards, TV and radio announcements, and wholesale distribution of literature. But this is not the case. While evangelism using mass media has its place, individual Christian witness is an even more effective means of reaching people for Christ.

God's intent in making you His witness is that others may come to know Jesus. But this doesn't mean that you are responsible to "convert" those with whom you come in contact. It is God's Holy Spirit who convicts (John 16:8); you and I as God's witnesses are only a part of His message. For this reason, I believe we should put more emphasis, in our Christian teaching, on *being* a witness than on *doing* witnessing. If you are enjoying God, the Holy Spirit will give you opportunities to share Him with others. But what you *are* will be more important to your non-Christian friends than what you *say*.

Paul wrote to the Christians at Philippi that they were to "shine like stars in the universe" (Philippians 2:15). Other translations read "lights." Whether we picture ourselves as stars with the capability of guiding travelers, or lamps in a dark room, the simile is a significant one. We are called to be guides and illuminants to those around us who do not know our Lord.

Here, as in other areas of the Christian life, the guidance of God's Holy Spirit is important. He is the divine witness on earth today (Acts 5:32). In revealing Christ to unsaved men and women, He speaks to them directly in many ways. In addition, since He knows the condition, attitude, and thoughts of each person with whom you come in contact, He can guide you so that you can be effective in helping to reach these individuals for Christ.

If you blunder along in your witnessing, operating in the

energy of the flesh, you may actually be a negative influence on those the Holy Spirit is trying to reach.

Some years ago, I invited to a church meeting a man with whom I worked. My guest was a sensitive and intelligent young architect who was just beginning to think through his need of God, and who was interested in learning more about Him. After the service, he was cornered by a zealous Christian who felt that all visitors should be "confronted with the claims of Christ." My friend was affronted by the steam-roller approach and his interest in the Christian faith was abruptly turned off—permanently as far as I know. While confrontation may sometimes be necessary, I suspect in this case the "witness" was guided by the flesh.

As this example also shows, an effective witness must use intelligence and common sense in presenting the gospel. If you would influence others for Christ, you must first become a friend, sincerely, not just as a tactic to assist your witness. To put it another way, you must often build solid bridges from your life to the lives of others before you can bring them spiritual aid. The principles found in 1 Corinthians 9:19-20 and Matthew 10:16 can also help you here.

If you are yielded to God, the Holy Spirit can bring you into direct contact with those for whom your personal witness can be most effective. He can influence you in the small matters of dress, casual conversation, and action so that in all these things you will be a testimony to those around you. He will so shine in your life that they will catch a glimpse of Christ in you. And when the opportunity to speak of Jesus comes, He can be depended on to guide your thoughts and your words.

Guidance in Priestly Service

Every Christian is a priest (1 Peter 2:9). A priest is someone who has direct access to God, and this access is closely related to the subject of guidance.

A priest has access to God through worship. God seeks worshipers, as Jesus Himself tells us (John 4:23), and it is by God's Spirit that you are able to worship Him. Two of several words translated "worship" in our English Bible mean simply "to bow down to." You are worshiping God when you bow in spirit in His presence, recognizing Him for who He is, and thanking Him for what He has done in your life. You can worship in private prayer, or with other believers. A communion service where Christians gather to remember the Lord Jesus with symbols of bread and wine is a special time of worship. As you worship, you can ask, as David did, that your words and thoughts will be acceptable to God (Psalm 19:14). You can be sure that the Holy Spirit who indwells you will guide you so that you will be able to worship intelligently.

The process of worshiping God can also, by drawing you closer to Him, make you more sensitive and sure about His purposes in the world. David was troubled because wicked men seemed to prosper until he spent time in God's sanctuary, the place of worship. Then he began to understand that the success of those who rejected God was only temporary (Psalm 73:3,17). You will acquire a better understanding of God's will as you spend time worshiping Him.

As a priest, you also have the privilege of bringing requests to God. You can ask Him to meet your own needs, and you can also represent other people before God. Those Christian friends who are sick or in financial straits are certainly praying on their own account, but you can step in with your prayers to help carry their burden. And what about acquaintances who don't know your God? While they can't pray, in any real way, for their own needs, you can pray for them.

It may seem strange that you should ask God to guide you in your asking, but the Bible implies just that. The apostle

John stressed the importance of asking "according to his will" (1 John 5:14). In other words, your attitude and thoughts should be in tune with God's purposes as you pray. As in the case of other daily decisions, being guided to pray in God's will is not a matter of looking for signs. If you commit yourself and your priestly responsibilities to God, you can pray confidently, expecting Him to guide you. As with other guidance experiences, this is a learning process. The Holy Spirit may begin bringing to your mind specific situations and individuals to pray for. He will sometimes even give you a conviction that you should stop praying about a certain matter.

Asking God to guide your prayers does not guarantee that each request will be answered at once, or that the answer, when it comes, will be the one you want and expect. You must allow God to handle the situations you pray about in His own way. But if you let God's Holy Spirit participate fully in your prayer life, He has promised that He will pray within you and for you (Romans 8:26-27), with the result that your prayers, even your unspoken ones, will be meaningful and effective.

Guidance in Christian Relationships

When you and I became Christians, we also became, automatically, members of the universal company of brothers and sisters in Christ (Matthew 23:8). The apostle Paul put it another way: "We were all baptized by one Spirit into one body" (1 Corinthians 12:13). This body is the church. You will never meet on this earth most of the members of God's universal church—some live far away, and others are already in heaven—but you will find yourself in contact with those believers who live or work near you, or who are associated with the same local church.

You are responsible, the Bible says, to be a functioning

member of this body, a true sister or brother in the faith to other Christians. You need God's guidance to be able to give these other believers the affection and support they need.

There are various responsibilities that God gives you in connection with other Christians:

1. You are to love them (1 John 3:14).
2. You are to pray for them (James 5:16).
3. You are to be selfless in serving them (John 13:14-15).
4. You are to stand ready to bear their burdens (take their troubles on yourself) when necessary (Galatians 6:2).
5. You are to be willing even to lay down your own life for them, should the occasion demand it (1 John 3:16).

Your responsibility for these Christians has nothing at all to do with whether or not you find them attractive. Human love needs a response to make it worthwhile. God's love, which flows through us (Romans 5:5), works because of who God is, not because the person who is its object is lovable.

Does God's guidance fit into this picture? It certainly does. It is God's Spirit who molds individual Christians into a single body, and who sees to it that the various members of the body support each other. As you submit to His guidance He will help you to be of help to your brothers and sisters in Christ. You will find also (for all of God's requirements are two-way streets) that these other Christians will be a blessing to you.

As you go on in the path of faith, you will see repeated examples of the ways in which God guides Christians to help and support each other. Even small incidents can show God's care in a delightful way. For example, some time ago, my traveling companions and I were preparing to leave a distant city for the long drive home when we inadvertently locked the car keys in the trunk of the automobile. It was late Sunday afternoon with no commercial garages open nearby. But God had a solution ready. A Christian mechanic who "happened" to have his complete tool kit with him, stepped forward, and through his help the keys were soon recovered. More recently, some of us have been praying about the future of a young Christian couple who are moving to a part of the country where they know no one. While I was on a business trip God brought me in unexpected contact with a mature and spiritual Christian family who live in the very area to which these young people are moving. As a result, they are now assured of a welcome and an immediate introduction into an active church near their new home.

It is possible to view these happenings, and ones like them, as fortunate accidents. As believers we see in them the assurance of a wise and loving God that we are truly joined together in one body.

A special way in which you can interact with other Christians is through the development and use of your spiritual gift. I will talk about this subject in the next chapter.

QUESTIONS

1. What is the three-part mission every Christian has been given?

2. While God uses many means to spread the gospel, what are some of the advantages of a person-to-person witness over the use of mass advertising?

3. What can you learn from the fact that the Bible says more about being a witness than about doing witnessing? How does the picture of the believer as a star in the universe (Philippians 2:15) help in understanding this concept?

4. In what ways can God's Holy Spirit guide your witness? What are the dangers in attempting to be a witness without His guidance?

5. How can you apply the teaching of 1 Corinthians 9:19-20 and Matthew 10:16 in reaching others for Christ?

6. What are the functions of a priest? What are some ways in which each Christian can serve as a priest of God?

7. What are some of the practical ways in which God can guide individuals in priestly activities?

8. What are some responsibilities that you have with regard to other Christians?

9. How can the truth of Romans 5:5 help you to respond in a loving and helpful way, even to Christians you may dislike?

10. How does God's guidance help to draw Christians together? What role did divine guidance play in the two illustrations of Christian helpfulness near the end of this chapter?

CHAPTER 9

God's Will and Your Spiritual Gift

Have you been thinking of spiritual gifts as abilities that only professional preachers or fulltime Christian workers have? If so, you have missed one of the most fascinating ideas in the entire Bible: that Christianity is a fellowship of brothers and sisters, each of whom has a different spiritual ability, which is to be used for the benefit of all. Scripture says: "Each one should use whatever gift he has received to serve others, faithfully administering God's grace in its various forms" (1 Peter 4:10). • This and other verses indicate that you, as a believer in Christ, have a spiritual gift, and are responsible to use it. Just as you need God's guidance to serve Him as a witness, as a priest, and as a member of His family, you need His help in developing and using your gift. • Gifts are spiritual capabilities that the Lord has given to believers to develop and use in His service. The Greek word for gift in this passage is *charisma* (plural *charismata*) from which our English word *charismatic* comes. It means "a gift or favor graciously given," and is related to the word *charis,* meaning "grace." Each gift is just that: a favor from God, a bonus added by Him to the wonderful gift of salvation.

For a clearer idea of the operation of gifts, think for a moment about what the earliest churches, those we read about in the book of Acts, were like. There was, so far as we know, no single "pastor" or "minister" in any of these churches. The apostles and teachers who worked among the believers traveled from place to place, encouraging and building up the churches, but the week-in, week-out ministry of each church was carried on by its members. The idea that a resident, ordained clergyman was needed to direct and lead the spiritual program came later.

Each local body functioned as a group of brothers and sisters, working together under the guidance of elders appointed from its membership. Every Christian, they were assured, had a spiritual gift, provided by God, and these gifts enabled all members to contribute effectively to the spiritual program of the church. God in His wisdom saw to it that the needed variety of gifts was present in each local group.

Whether or not your local church, or mine, retains the features of these early congregations, spiritual gifts are as important now to church life and growth as they were in the days of Paul. God holds each of us responsible to know his gift and to use it for Him.

The topic of spiritual gifts is not a simple one. Like other complex biblical truths it has been subjected to differing interpretations. A thorough study of the gifts, including a review of these differences, is beyond the scope of this book. The purpose here is to identify the relationship between spiritual gifts and God's guidance.

However, it is important to begin with an understanding of what gifts are all about. In the rest of this chapter I will summarize the subject from my own perspective. The next chapter will suggest how God's guidance can help you find your spiritual gift.

Lists of the Gifts

Figure 1

1 Romans 12:6-8	2 1 Corinthians 12:8-10	3 1 Corinthians 12:28-30	4 Ephesians 4:11
Prophecy	Message of wisdom	Apostles	Apostles
Service	Message of knowledge	Prophets	Prophets
Teaching	Faith	Teachers	Evangelists
Encouraging	Healing	Miracle workers	Pastors
Giving	Miraculous powers	Healers	Teachers
Leadership	Prophecy	Helpers	
Showing mercy	Distinguishing between spirits	Administrators	
	Speaking in tongues	Speakers in tongues	
	Interpretation of tongues	Interpreters	

There are four passages in the New Testament that contain lists of gifts. They are found in three letters written by the apostle Paul, each to a different local church. These lists with scripture references are shown in Figure 1. The gifts in lists 1 and 2 in this table refer to the *charismata* themselves; those in lists 3 and 4 describe the persons who possess these qualities. These persons are also called "gifts" (Ephesians 4:8), but in a different sense. As they use the individual gifts God has given them, they become Christ's gifts to the church. (The Greek word for gift in this case is not *charisma* but *doma*, meaning simply "something given.")

List 1 is contained in Romans 12:6-8. "We have different gifts, according to the grace given us," Paul wrote to the Roman Christians. "If a man's [person's] gift is prophesying, let him use it in proportion to his faith. If it is serving, let him serve; if it is teaching, let him teach . . . " The basic message is clear: each believer is responsible to develop and utilize his or her gift.

List 2 is found in the early part of 1 Corinthians 12, the epistle written by Paul to the confused and immature Christians of Corinth. In this case his purpose was not to encourage them to use their gifts—they were already more than active in this regard—but to explain that the bestowal of gifts was under the control of the Holy Spirit. He introduced this second list with the statement, "Now to each one the manifestation of the Spirit is given for the common good," and ended with the words, "All these are the work of one and the same Spirit, and he gives them to each one, just as he determines."

List 3 is located at the end of this same chapter. It presents God the Father as the member of the godhead who assigns gifted individuals to their places of service in the church. Verse 28 reads, "And in the church, God has appointed first of all apostles, second prophets . . . "

List 4 is presented in the fourth chapter of Ephesians, a

book that explains the great truths of Christ's church. As in list 3, the gifts to be given are people. Through His death, resurrection, and ascension, Christ has become the giver of these benefits to the church. Verse 11 reads, "It was he [Christ] who gave some to be apostles, some to be prophets, some to be evangelists, and some to be pastors and teachers."

Do you see the pattern of responsibility that emerges? Lists 2, 3, and 4 show that each of the three members of the trinity is involved in the distribution and operation of gifts, a fact that affirms the importance of these wonderful spiritual enablements in the divine program. Romans 12, which contains list 1, emphasizes your duty and mine as believers to develop and use these gifts.

A Closer Look at the Gifts

Let's consider some of the questions that are often asked about spiritual gifts:

A talented person is often referred to as "gifted." Is there a difference between talents and spiritual gifts?

Yes, talents are natural abilities, possessed by Christians and non-Christians alike. We may use them for our own profit, or for the Lord. Gifts, on the other hand, are given only to believers, and by their nature are usable only in God's service.

What about musicians or artists whose principal way of serving God is through their talents? Aren't talents and gifts the same thing in this case?

No. While the talent may be a major factor in fulfilling one's spiritual gift, it is not the gift itself. A pianist whose primary ministry is playing for Sunday school or church services may correctly view music as a part of a gift of service, and a chalk artist may express a gift of evangelism through art. On the other hand there may be those who use their artistic talents for the Lord, but who find their gifts in quite different areas.

I notice you talk about an individual's "gift" rather than "gifts." Isn't it possible for me to have several gifts?

While the idea that every Christian has a number of gifts is a popular one, one-gift-to-a-customer appears to be God's normal plan. Each of the scripture passages in which gifts are mentioned seems to support this interpretation. The discourse centering around list 1 is aimed at encouraging each Christian to concentrate on one gift. In the list 2 passage we are told that the Spirit gives a different gift to each person. The scripture portions providing lists 3 and 4 make clear that gifts of apostleship and teaching and pastoring and evangelism are resident in different persons. In Paul's letters to Timothy he exhorted the younger man to stir up his *gift*, not his *gifts* (1 Timothy 4:14; 2 Timothy 1:6), and the passage in 1 Peter quoted earlier (4:10) states that each of us has received a gift (singular). None of the "gift passages" suggests in any way that a person may have multiple gifts.

Then how do you explain those Christians who are good at many things?

It is a mistake to think that whatever someone does well must be his or her gift. As we shall see, many of the names of gifts describe things that all Christians should do. Your own gift, however—the capability God has decreed for you—fits you for the thing that you will do best. It is a great tragedy when Christians spread themselves over so many areas of service that they never develop their unique gift to its full potential.

Each list in Figure 1 contains a slightly different set of gifts. How many gifts are there altogether?

Not everyone agrees on the total number. There are obvious duplications, as well as some additional possible gifts. There may also be God-given gifts not on any of the lists, though the thirty entries in these four passages seem to cover most of the qualities we see in action in the church today.

My own study has led me to settle on fifteen gifts, eliminating both obvious duplications and cases in which a gift in one list appears to be described in different terms in one or more of the other lists. These fifteen are identified in Figure 2 and the definitions that follow.

Are all of these fifteen gifts active today?

Opinions also differ on this question. I seriously doubt that the four supernatural "sign" gifts (miracles, healing, tongues, interpretation of tongues) are now in use. It is possible, I believe, to identify in the church today, all of the other gifts listed.

History shows that God has limited His special signs, His spectacular public miracles, to certain times and places. For example, there were many supernatural signs during Israel's journey from Egypt but comparatively few in the centuries before and afterward. Miracles were abundant during the earthly ministry of Jesus and the apostolic period that followed, but have been rare since that time.

I am aware that some claim to have these "sign" gifts today. However, the evidence seems to show that the Lord is more interested now in carrying out His work in other, more quiet ways. Until we see convincing indications of "sign" gifts which function as described in the New Testament, and which produce the unmistakably genuine results we read about in the Bible, we are entitled to reserve judgment on claims that the public signs of the first century are again among us.

At the other end of the spectrum are those who see evidence in New Testament scriptures that certain gifts were to cease at a specific time in history. In particular, 1 Corinthians 13:10 has been taken to mean that the miracle gifts were to terminate when the New Testament was completed, and Ephesians 2:20, that the gifts of apostle and prophet were to be withdrawn after the church age began. In neither case is the proof convincing, and in both cases there are other equally plausible interpretations. These issues are discussed in more detail in Notes 3 and 4.

Definitions of Gifts

While the Bible does not give specific definitions, we can get an idea of the function of the gifts by what the scriptures do say about them.

Figure 2

The Fifteen Gifts

The Seven Gifts in List 1	Gifts Not in List 1 but in One or More of the Other Lists	
	Non-Sign Gifts	*Sign Gifts*
Prophecy	Faith	Healing
Service	Discerning spirits	Miracle working
Teaching	Apostleship	Speaking in tongues
Encouraging	Evangelism	Interpretation of
Giving		tongues
Leadership		
Showing mercy		

Prophecy: The gift of sharing with others helpful spiritual revelations from God's word. We sometimes think of prophets as foretellers of future events. While Old Testament prophets predicted the future on occasion, their principal role was expressing whatever truth God chose to reveal. In these days revelation comes through God's word. While we all may read the Bible for ourselves, God gives some the special gift of bringing to His people practical and timely insights from the word, which meet exactly the need of the moment. People so gifted may well be thought of as present-day prophets. 1 Corinthians 14:3 and 2 Peter 1:19 describe the value and effect of prophecy. See Note 3.

Service (Helper in list 3): The gift of seeing the need for practical help, and giving this help. All of us know Christians who have an outstanding quality of recognizing jobs to be done and setting to work joyfully with hands, brains, and tools to accomplish them for Christ. People with special talents in music, art, or craftsmanship are often, though not always, those with a gift of service. While all Christians are called to serve, those with this special gift provide the inspirational examples of selfless service that the rest of us need.

Teaching (Message of knowledge in list 2): The gift of understanding and expounding the scriptures. It seems reasonable to consider teaching and message of knowledge as the same gift. This gift deals with God's word, as does prophecy. However, the approach in each case is different. The prophet shares God's revelations as he receives them. The teacher, on the other hand, studies and presents doctrinal truth in an organized, systematic fashion. His gift lies in making the "message of knowledge" available in clear and understandable form to others in the body of Christ. On the basis of grammatical construction in Ephesians 4, some maintain that pastor/teacher is a single composite gift. However, in my view the evidence is less than convincing. See Note 5 for additional discussion of this point.

Encouraging (Message of wisdom in list 2; Pastor in list 4): The gift of caring for, guiding, and supporting other Christians. The Greek word translated "exhorting" (KJV) has also the broader meanings of "encouraging" and "comforting." I see this gift as probably identical with the "message of wisdom" and almost surely the same as the gift of "pastor." Today many think of a pastor as a clergyman but this is not the true meaning of the term. (As I noted earlier, there is no evidence that New Testament churches had specially ordained resident preachers.) *Pastor* means shepherd. God's intent is that each church has within it a group of members whose special gift lies in shepherding those younger or weaker in the faith. Scripturally, we can apply the title "pastor" to a teenage girl who serves as a spiritual guide for small children as well as to a mature counselor of adult Christians. Pastors are concerned with encouraging people and building them up spiritually. However, like the teachers and the prophets they must be well-versed in scripture. From the Bible they draw the "word of wisdom" suited to the particular need of the persons with whom they are dealing. (Note 6 also applies.)

Giving: The gift of supporting God's work through wise donation of money or material goods. This is an important gift requiring sensitivity to needs and humbleness of spirit. In some cases those with this gift may be given great wealth to use for God; in other cases they may be people of modest means whose ability to give effectively and willingly is such that it inspires and encourages others in this responsibility.

Leadership; (Administrator in list 3): The gift of planning, organizing, and directing Christian work. Some who have this gift today can be found in executive posts in large Christian organizations. Others serve in local churches, where they function effectively in supervising many types of church programs.

Truly gifted leaders get jobs done and, more importantly, help those who serve with them to recognize each task as a spiritual experience.

Showing mercy: The gift of expressing lovingkindness to those who need it. Much of the trouble among Christians begins with inner feelings of anger, guilt, hurt, or frustration. Such feelings may be acknowledged or hidden under protective shells of cynical or aggressive behavior. This gift is concerned with healing the wounds that result from these feelings and with restoring true unity in the body of Christ.

Faith: The gift of trusting God in trying circumstances. This is not simply an intensification of the faith common to all Christians but unusual faith required to meet difficult situations in the world. Those with this gift are especially called by God to carry on His work under discouraging conditions, or to accomplish great things for Him through faith.

Discerning spirits: The gift of separating manifestations of the Holy Spirit from Satan's counterfeits. Those with this capability can see through the devices of the enemy to distinguish false spiritual motivation from true, and to unmask heretical cults. They can also make the difficult distinction between honest differences in interpretation of scripture and dangerous false teaching.

Apostleship: The gift of founding local churches in new areas. The word apostle means "sent one." The apostles chosen by Jesus personally were sent out to become founders of the early churches. These were followed by other apostles whose names are given in the book of Acts and the epistles. While all Christians are sent into the world to fulfill the great commission, some in every age of the church are called to be human catalysts around whom new church testimonies can grow. These can appropriately be called apostles. See Note 3.

Evangelism: The gift of bringing uncommitted persons to the point of accepting Christ as Savior. An evangelist may be either a preacher to large audiences, or one who deals personally with individuals. Every Christian is a witness, but not all are evangelists. The goal of a witness is to share one's faith with the non-Christian; the function of one with an evangelistic gift is to be the open channel through which the Holy Spirit brings about the conversion of the unbeliever. The responsibility of a Christian witness, like that of a witness in a court of law, is to present what he knows of the truth; the mission of an evangelist is similar to that of a trial lawyer who marshals the evidence in convincing form to bring about a correct verdict.

The Four "Sign" Gifts: These gifts constitute special signs given to demonstrate God's power to an unbelieving world. They include: healing: the gift of healing human ailments by miraculous means; miracle working: the gift of calling forth miraculous signs; speaking in tongues: the gift of speaking in a language that has not been learned; interpretation of tongues: the gift of understanding and explaining what is spoken by a tongues-speaker.

QUESTIONS

1. Why is it important to the functioning of a healthy Christian church that the members have differing spiritual gifts?

2. What responsibility does 1 Peter 4:10 give you with respect to your spiritual gift?

3. How do the four gift passages in the New Testament show that all three members of the trinity are interested in the operation of spiritual gifts?

4. How do gifts and natural talents differ? How may a person's natural talent support his or her spiritual gift?

5. What are some of the statements in scripture which point to the conclusion that one-gift-to-a-person is God's normal rule?

6. If God gives one gift per person, how is it that certain Christians seem to be good at many things?

7. The gifts of prophecy, teaching, and encouraging are all "speaking" gifts. How do these gifts differ?

8. How does the scriptural use of the term prophet differ from the popular idea about this term?

9. What is the difference between the way the term pastor is applied in many churches today, and its scriptural meaning?

10. The gifts of serving, giving, leading, and showing mercy are "action" gifts. How do these gifts differ from each other?

CHAPTER 10

Finding Your Spiritual Gift

Look again at Romans 12, the Bible passage that contains list 1. Since it emphasizes your responsibilities as individuals to use your gift, it is an appropriate place to start. • In Chapter 4 of this book, we learned that the initial verses of Romans 12 give us a three-step approach to knowing God's will. These steps lead directly to the list of spiritual gifts in verses 6-8. The steps are: • 1. Make a definite prayerful decision each day to "offer your body" to God. Put your future in His hands (Romans 12:1). • 2. Don't let the world's way of life, its ambitions, its attractions, get a strangle-hold on your life; "renew" your mind each day through prayer and the reading of God's word (Romans 12:2a). • 3. God will then reveal His perfect will in your life (Romans 12:2b). • That is where we stopped in Chapter 4. As we read further in Romans 12 we find three more steps in knowing God's will in our service for Him. • 4. Establish a right view of yourself. Recognize that your life is important to God, but don't allow pride or self-importance to mar your service for Him (Romans 12:3). • 5. Establish a right view of your fellow Christians. Remember that each believer is a part of Christ's body, designed to function as a unit with all parts working together for the benefit of all (Romans 12:4-5).

6. Recognize that your gift is already within you, placed there by the indwelling Spirit (Romans 12:6).

At this point the apostle Paul launched into the list of gifts, with the admonition that each Christian should put his or her gift to use. There is no formula for recognizing which gift is yours, but then God hasn't operated by formula in any of the other areas of guidance we have studied. His way of teaching is through on-the-job training.

Each of the seven gifts in Romans 12 (Figure 1) is something that provides direct spiritual support to the members of the local church. Also, as we read through the New Testament epistles, we find that each gift is something which every Christian should practice. For example, all Christians are encouraged to prophesy (1 Corinthians 14:31). They are to serve one another (Galatians 6:2), teach one another (Colossians 3:16), encourage one another (1 Thessalonians 5:11), contribute money and time to God's work (1 Corinthians 16:2), lead and motivate others in right directions (Hebrews 10:24), and show mercy (Ephesians 4:32).

Do you see how this truth fits in with what you have learned about God's OJT program? As you practice these virtues faithfully, God will make it clear, sooner or later, which one is your special spiritual gift.

An illustration may help. When my son went out for Little League baseball some years ago, he found that the manager wanted every boy to work out at all of the positions. Each spent practice time shagging flies in the outfield, handling infield grounders, pitching, and catching. As time went on, it became apparent to both the players and the manager exactly how the talents of each boy could best be used.

God, of course, knows what gift He has given you. His OJT program will allow you to find it. Romans 12:11 describes the attitude with which He wants you to pursue this program. It reads, "Never be lacking in zeal, but keep your spiritual fervor, serving the Lord."

We can now add four final points to our list of guidelines.

7. Practice all of the seven types of Christian activity listed in verses 6-8—prophecy, serving, teaching, encouraging, contributing, leading, showing mercy—as opportunity offers. Accept each opportunity to serve in these ways as from the Lord.

8. Evaluate prayerfully your performance in these activities, asking God to guide you to your specific gift.

9. If one kind of service proves to be particularly fulfilling and effective, begin concentrating more of your efforts in that direction.

10. As this process of serving and learning proceeds, expect God to begin to confirm your gift through one or more of the means of guidance we have already discussed. If you see positive results from one particular kind of ministry, if other spiritual Christians begin to recognize it as "your thing," accept it as God's gift for you.

Has this approach proved itself in practice? Many times over. I think of a young man who began by giving God priority in his life. He became active in witnessing, a willing church worker, and a participant in church prayer and worship functions. Of the many jobs given him as youth teacher, organizer of youth activities, and camp counselor, he found that he was particularly successful in advising and counseling younger Christians. After a time of prayer and self-evaluation, he asked to be relieved of certain organizational assignments at the Christian camp where he served, so that he could be more available for one-on-one counseling work. He has concluded that he has a pastoral gift.

Had this young man sat still and prayed for the Lord to

show him his area of service he might still be uncertain about it. Because he was willing to learn by doing, the Holy Spirit was able to lead him to his own unique gift.

What about the Other Gifts?

Suppose your gift is not one of these seven in Romans 12? The remaining eight, listed in Figure 2, are of a different sort. They are each aimed at dealing, in one way or another, with the world outside of our Christian fellowship. Thus, special faith is a means of overcoming the trials and disasters that come through circumstances; the discernment of spirits is related to the subtle attacks of the enemy; apostleship and evangelism are concerned with the spread of the gospel to the world; and the miracle gifts, as they were used in New Testament times, were special signs for unbelievers.

We have already suggested that the gifts of special faith—discerning of spirits, apostleship, and evangelism—are active today. However, they are not routinely used within local congregations as are the gifts of list 1. Therefore, if God has one of these gifts for you, the steps in discovering it will be different.

While the principle of learning while doing still applies, these gifts cannot be practiced in normal church life. While you exercise faith in God every day, you cannot exercise the kind of trust embodied in the gift of faith unless God places you in the circumstances that require it. You may distinguish false influences from true in your daily life but a major spiritual conflict is probably required to make the gift of discerning spirits recognizable. You can serve as a witness to unbelievers, and desire to see new churches established, but if you have the gift of apostleship or evangelism, you will be called, empowered, and placed where these gifts are needed.

Identification of these gifts is likely to come about in the following way:

1. Though you continue to serve in the areas listed in Romans 12, you will not find complete fulfillment and satisfaction in them. You will develop no special spiritual capability in any of them.

2. As you pray for God's will to be done in your life, you will sooner or later be placed in a situation where you will recognize a special call from God, or where circumstances will make the exercise of your gift natural and right.

3. You will be given confidence to exercise this gift and will use it effectively.

4. Other discerning Christians will recognize and accept your gift for what it is.

Suppose, for example, God wants you to be an evangelist (a call to apostleship, faith, or discerning of spirits would follow a similar pattern). Evangelists may be either preachers who bring the gospel to thousands, or men and women who specialize in one-on-one ministry. Whichever God wants you to be, you will find yourself more interested in reaching the unconverted with the gospel than in interacting with other Christians. You will be placed in circumstances where you can lead people to Christ. God will give you the words to bring them to a decision. Other Christians will recognize you as an evangelist.

The "Sign" Gifts Again

It is interesting to note that the four "sign" gifts, like the gifts we have just considered, had their focus outside the church. Many of those who desperately want to speak in tongues today think of this and other signs as spiritual abilities to be used in normal church life. The apostle Paul pointed out, however, that they were primarily for unbelievers and were not for display among Christians (1 Corinthians 14:22).

It seems reasonable to think of such signs as special demonstrations to validate God's message. As such they were particularly useful in the early days of the faith, as a means of calling attention to the vibrant new gospel. If God were again to choose to use "sign" gifts, now or in the future, we should expect them to follow the pattern of gifts not in list 1; that is, those to be gifted would be put in the special circumstances where signs were required and power would be given, probably suddenly, to meet the need.

You and I should not beg God for signs, or struggle to acquire miraculous gifts. We should concentrate on gifts of spiritual substance, leaving the giving of signs where it must be—in the hand of God.

In Summary

We have learned in this chapter that finding your gift is not a mysterious thing, but a process much like seeking God's will in any other matter. The keynotes are yielding to God, following spiritual principles in a logical way, and being ready to recognize His answer when it comes. The development of your gift will take time. Serve Him, in whatever ways you can, and let Him reveal your gift when He is ready to do so.

Bear in mind that your gift, whatever it may be, can be used wherever the Lord puts you. If, for example, your gift is prophecy, you may be led to exercise it before large audiences, as a member of a discussion group, or in informal conversations. A Sunday school teacher may have the gift of teaching or encouraging or evangelism. The important thing is not that the "label" fits. It is that you are comfortable in what God has called you to do.

It is possible that the final niche in which God puts you may not relate to any of the gifts I have described. While I have thus far been able to fit all of the kinds of Christian service I have seen into one of the fifteen categories, I would not restrict God dogmatically to this list. If He has something totally different in mind for you, He will give you unmistakable guidance. You cannot limit God, but you can count on Him to make your way certain.

God's View of the Gifts

Finally, let's stand back and look at the entire subject of gifts from a slightly different angle. Jesus Christ was the only person who ever displayed the gifts fully in His own person. He was an apostle, a prophet, a shepherd, a teacher, and all the rest. He has gone to heaven, leaving us here as His representatives. Our job is to let Him live in our lives, so that those around will see Him in us. But none of us individually has the capacity to represent Him.

That's where the gifts come in. Ephesians 4:13 tells us that the purpose of the gifts is that we, as a group or body, might grow to "the whole measure of the fullness of Christ." Each of us has a different gift so that each can show one aspect of the quality of Jesus better than anyone else. And all the Christians together—the whole glorious body—can, through their different gifts, show a multidimensional view of Jesus Christ so that others may know what He is really like. What better incentive can you and I have for developing our gift?

QUESTIONS

1. Which of the fifteen gifts described in this chapter directly support other members of the body of Christ?

2. Which of these gifts appear to be aimed more specifically at the world outside our Christian fellowship?

3. Why does the list in Romans 12 prove the best starting point for finding your gift?

4. Assuming your spiritual gift is one of those listed in Romans 12, what are the three steps listed in verses 1 and 2 that you should take in order to discover and use this gift for God?

5. What are the next three steps (Romans 12:3-6)?

6. What are the final four suggested steps in this process?

7. What are four principles that may help you decide whether or not your gift is one of the eight that are used primarily outside the church?

8. Why is it appropriate that the four "sign" gifts are found in the category to be used outside the church?

9. Should you be concerned if you are not able to identify your gift immediately? Why or why not?

10. According to Ephesians 4:13, what is one purpose of spiritual gifts? How do all of the gifts together help in the presentation of Jesus Christ to the world?

CHAPTER 11

God's Will and Your Career

One of life's major decisions is the choice of a vocation. "What are you going to be?" is one of the easiest questions to ask, and often one of the hardest to answer. • A few generations ago, when most women became fulltime homemakers, this chapter might have been of interest only to men. However, in today's world most women work outside the home for at least a few years before marrying, and many, often because of economic necessity, return to the work force after marriage. Careers in business, industry, and the professions are now open to people of both genders. While fulltime homemaking remains the first choice for many women, others in increasing numbers are pursuing outside careers. • I find no prohibition in scripture against any of these options. The important thing is that, whether you are a male or female Christian, you seek God's guidance in determining your role in life. • How should you as a Christian decide on your life's work? Some verses from the first book of Corinthians can give you a starting point: "Each one should remain in the situation which he was in when God called him. Were you a slave when you were called? Don't let it trouble you—although if you can gain your freedom, do so. For he who was a slave when he was called by the Lord is the Lord's freedman; similarly, he who was a free man when he was called is Christ's slave. You were bought at a price; do not become slaves of men. Brothers, each man, as responsible to God, should remain in the situation God called him to" (1 Corinthians 7:20-24).

In reading this passage, remember that selecting a vocation was not the major problem in New Testament times (or in most other ages) that it is now. In many cases the choice didn't exist. People were farmers or carpenters or house servants because it was the traditional vocation of their family or because circumstances forced them in that direction. Also, in Bible times, most industry was home-based. There were many family businesses like those of Priscilla and Aquila (Acts 18:1-3) and Lydia (Acts 16:14). Children in such households learned the skills of their parents, and used these skills as adults. It is likely, for example, that the apostle Paul was a tentmaker because his father was. Under these circumstances, it is understandable that he should stress the need for Christians to be content with their lot rather than how to choose it.

However, this scripture also has something to say in today's world, where there is a choice of vocations. It points out that your present vocation or place in life is an assignment (what a military man would call a "duty station") given you by God. Accepting this assignment opens the way to a close relationship with Him in your daily work. The first century slave could assure himself, as he went about his labors, that he was "the Lord's freedman," and the free man was reminded that he was "Christ's slave." In both cases, they were to remember that God was with them in their vocations. In the same way, whether you are a homemaker, a student, or an executive, you should consider yourself to be God's person, occupying the place He has planned for you.

It follows that you should not spend your time scheming and planning to "get ahead," as the non-Christian often does. However, when choices are available you should use them wisely. "Were you a slave when you were called? Don't let it trouble you—although if you can gain your freedom, do so" (1 Corinthians 7:21). Since your circumstances are a part of God's "assignment," you must be content with them, but you can look on any reasonable opportunity to improve things as also from Him.

Suppose, for example, you are prevented from completing your education through illness or lack of funds. It is natural and right for you to hope to go back to school, and to look for ways of accomplishing this, but it is also expected of you as a Christian that you be content where you are until God sees fit to open the way. "I have learned to be content whatever the circumstances" (Philippians 4:11), said Paul, and while he spoke in a different context we can apply his attitude to our career problems.

When it comes to choosing your vocation, you should apply the principles for decision-making we have already discussed. Start with basic guidelines. The Bible contains many principles that can influence your choice. For example, your life-work should be fundamentally good (3 John 11), and you should not be unequally "yoked" with unbelievers (2 Corinthians 6:14).

The first of these concepts would, for instance, rule out a job peddling pornographic literature, even though under our present laws such sales might be entirely legal. The second should cause you to look carefully at any vocational opportunity in which you would become closely identified with non-Christians under circumstances that might hinder your testimony. Some Christians feel that 2 Corinthians 6:14 rules out business partnerships of any kind between Christians and non-Christians. However, others feel that certain legal partnerships, properly drawn up, are no more a "yoke" than any other type of contract. Each such situation must be judged on its own merits.

First Steps

There are some positive steps you can take toward finding your life's vocation. Before surveying secular careers, you should seriously consider whether or not the Lord wants you to enter fulltime Christian service. With the rapid escalation in world population, there are increasing needs for Christian workers at home and abroad. Many of these needs can best be filled by dedicated men and women in fulltime service. Yet we are told that a smaller percentage of young people are choosing Christian service as a career today than in the past. The fact that you may intend, if you follow a business career, to give a great deal of money to the Lord's work is not the real issue. The issue is whether or not you really mean it when you say, "God's will be done." If so, the only pertinent question is: "What does He want me to be?"

Some young people feel that unless they are especially gifted as preachers or teachers, a career in fulltime service for the Lord is not for them. However, a look at the needs for personnel in foreign missions and domestic Christian activities will lay this idea to rest. In this technical age, the Lord has fulltime use for pilots, doctors, nurses, writers, mechanics, secretaries, accountants, librarians, translators, hospital administrators, and many other specialists.

Fulltime Christian service is not easy. It requires a willingness to sacrifice, a complete dedication to God's work, and possibly physical hardship. As a Christian worker, you may never be rich in an earthly sense. However, the spiritual rewards of those the Lord calls to such service are great.

Other Important Factors

Once you are clear on the scriptural guidelines, and determined to follow God's will for your life wherever this may lead, you can begin considering specific factors. Three important ones are your natural aptitudes, your spiritual gift, and your opportunities. As you look at these factors in a careful, objective manner, you will give maximum scope for the use of your brains and common sense, and will also allow God, through His indwelling Holy Spirit, to begin influencing your thinking in the direction He has chosen.

Natural aptitudes are the physical and mental abilities with which you were born. The special aptitude test you take in school can help you understand your abilities, as can the interests you develop through hobbies and reading. If you find yourself beginning to think seriously about any one type of life-work as a result of recognizing your abilities, ask the Lord about it: "Is this the thing I should concentrate on, Lord? Show me Your will . . . "

The spiritual gift which the Lord has given you can also help determine your career. We have already talked about how to find your gift. If your purpose in life is service to God, the vocation He selects for you will not interfere with, and may be related to, your spiritual gift. If you are especially gifted as an evangelist or a teacher, this gift may be a factor in pointing you toward a fulltime career as a preacher or a missionary (although, as we have pointed out, the presence of a "preaching" gift doesn't automatically indicate fulltime service, nor does the absence of such a gift rule against fulltime service). It may be that the Lord will lead you to a secular environment where your gift can be used for Him. An interest in young people may lead to a career in school teaching, where your gift of evangelism or encouraging or teaching can find full scope.

Opportunities which arise are also often important indications of what God wants you to do. If, for example, you are planning to go to work after high school, but a college scholarship unexpectedly becomes available, take a fresh look at your plans. The Lord may be guiding you through either positive or negative circumstances. Opportunities must be evaluated in the light of your resources. If your parents are unable to pay your way through college, planning must keep this in mind. If you are the sole support of a dependent adult relative, it is possible that you can't conscientiously go off to the missionfield, unless the Lord relieves you of this responsibility.

In the final analysis, as the Lord leads you toward the career He has for you, you may expect to experience the guidance of peace of mind which will assure you that your choice has been right.

QUESTIONS

1. What is the probable reason why the Bible does not provide specific guidelines for choosing a vocation?

2. 1 Corinthians 7:20-24 deals with the need for Christians to be content with their vocations. How should this truth be applied in today's world, where many Christians have a choice of jobs?

3. Why does it help if you view your vocation as an "assignment" from God?

4. What truths, set forth in 3 John 11, 2 Corinthians 6:14, and Philippians 4:11, should influence your attitude as you seek the place in life God has for you?

5. Why is the problem of deciding whether or not a relationship with an unbeliever constitutes an unequal yoke particularly difficult in today's world? What are some relationships that would constitute an unequal yoke, and others that would not?

6. What are some positive reasons for considering fulltime Christian service as a career? In today's world how might such specialists as computer programmers, secretaries, plumbers, and construction engineers be used as fulltime Christian workers in domestic or foreign areas?

7. What attitudes must you have if you truly desire to learn whether or not God has called you to fulltime Christian service?

8. What are three important factors we should evaluate in seeking our vocation? How can each of these be used by God to guide us in making the right decision?

9. How might God use each of the methods of guidance described in Chapter 6 in directing a young Christian toward the vocation He wants him or her to have?

10. What significant events or turning points in your own life have helped to fit you for the place you now occupy?

CHAPTER 12

God's Will and Your Marriage

I f you are determined to put God first in your life, you can expect His guidance concerning whether to marry, when to marry, and whom to marry. • While for most Christian young people marrying is probably God's will, the Bible does point out that some serve the Lord more effectively by remaining single (1 Corinthians 7:25-35). As a single person, begin by putting into God's hands the question of whether or not to marry. If His will is that you stay single, He will let you know either by not providing the "right" person for you to marry, or by bringing you to a positive decision to remain single for His service. • If you have dreamed of a home and a family of your own, remaining single may seem a great deal for the Lord to ask of you. Jesus Himself indicated that giving up home and marriage for God's kingdom was indeed a major sacrifice, and promised that those who did sacrifice such cherished things would be specially rewarded (Mark 10:29-30). • At the same time, you should not jump to the conclusion that you are "called" to remain single without a great deal of prayer, and a real concern for knowing God's will in the matter. It would be just as big a mistake to disobey God by refusing to consider marriage if marriage were really His plan for you, as it would be to rush into a wedding against His will. There are many to whom God hasn't given the unique qualities of faith and stability necessary to a lifelong service for Him as an unmarried Christian.

Is There One "Right" Person?

Assuming that God intends for you to marry, does He have a specific partner picked out for you? This is an often-asked question. While there is no Bible verse that treats this subject directly, what we have learned from the scriptures about God's ways in guidance points clearly to a "yes" answer. The God who plans your life in detail is certainly concerned about whom you marry.

Many Christian young people who raise this question are afraid that they may somehow miss connections and marry the wrong person. To give in to such worries is really to doubt God, who has promised to guide you. Just as you trusted Him for salvation, you must trust Him in your Christian walk. If you put Him first, you can count on Him to lead you to the partner who is best for you.

Other Christians are concerned because they have already married without having made sure of God's guidance. If this is your situation, should you consider that your marriage, contracted before you were yielded to Him, linked you for life with the wrong person? Not at all. I will write more about the possibility of wrong choices in the next chapter. Here let me simply say that God, in His infinite foreknowledge, was aware, long ago, of what your present circumstances would be. And His will for you *now*—regardless of the past—is for you to serve Him where you are, and with the husband or wife that you now have.

Choosing a Mate

Some have wondered why Paul, who wrote a good bit about Christians and marriage, should have said nothing about how the Lord guides in choosing a wife or husband. In fact, Paul's statement concerning widows—"She is free to marry anyone she wishes, but he must belong to the Lord" (1 Corinthians 7:39)—has been cited by some to support the idea that God doesn't care whom you marry so long as the individual is a Christian. This conclusion, of course, does not follow from the passage, which is concerned only with instructing the Corinthian church as to the conditions under which a second marriage for a Christian was appropriate. The church had no responsibility to guide the widow's choice of a husband, and Paul made this principle clear. The decision of whom to marry was between the widow and the Lord.

There are several possible reasons why God hasn't treated in detail in the scriptures His process of guidance in choosing a life-partner. For one thing, the Bible tends to discuss principles, not specific cases. Decisions about marriage pose much the same problems as do other major decisions. Then, too, the Bible was written for all ages and cultures, and marriages have come about in many different ways during the world's history. Even today customs differ. Christian parents in India, for example, follow the cultural pattern of their country in arranging marriages for their children, while in western countries young people are usually free to choose their own mates.

Under any accepted social arrangement, the Christian can expect God to guide in the matter of marriage, as He does in other decisions. However, since most of us live in societies where decisions about marriage are made by the individuals concerned, we will discuss the problem from this point of view.

Why Two Heads Are Better Than One

There is a wonderful promise given by the Lord Jesus and recorded in the book of Matthew that states: "If two of you on earth agree about anything you ask for, it will be done for you by my Father in heaven" (Matthew 18:19).

One way to put this promise into action is for a Christian man and woman, who are seriously interested in each other, to pray together for God to show them whether or not they should marry.

Certainly this is a little different from the traditional idea of courtship, in which the young man waits until he is sure in his own mind about marrying, and then proposes. But then, the traditional form was designed by the world, where marriage is often a business of "catching" and "being caught." Courtship, to a spiritual Christian couple, is quite another matter. It can and should be a time for romance (in the best sense of that old-fashioned term), but it should also be a time for honesty, for frank discussion of the spiritual ambitions of each partner, and for mutual prayer. It is most important that you pray about that decision with the person you are thinking of marrying and about each of your individual ideas for the future. If your intended mate doesn't like the idea of spending time in prayer, this objection may tell you that you don't share the same spiritual interests. If he or she does pray with you, you can expect clear guidance for the way ahead. When, as a result of this kind of prayerful courtship, a couple decides to marry, they can be sure the decision is the right one. In addition, the habit of sharing spiritual experiences can grow from this beginning into the closest kind of spiritual harmony in marriage itself—the harmony of a husband and wife who realize that they are "heirs . . . of the gracious gift of life" (1 Peter 3:7). There is no better human partnership.

The process of reaching the right decision is no different

in the case of marriage from any other important matter. Willingness to let God's will be done, consideration of the pros and cons, and prayer about each part of the problem—all are important. Areas of possible incompatibility—the ways in which each partner irritates or grates on the other—should be thoroughly talked over and prayed about. Hopes and plans for the future should be aired and compared. As you consider these factors, and as you pray, God will point you toward the decision that reflects His will for you.

How does romantic love fit into this process? Love is often the most wonderful "indicator" of all as to what God's will is. If your proposed marriage is in the will of God, your love for each other will not only grow as you pray together, but will draw each of you closer to God, so that your greatest joy together will be in worshiping and serving Him.

Single Life before Marriage

If you are sure that God has called you to remain single, you are free to dismiss marriage from your mind and concentrate on the Christian service He has for you. However, if you do not have this assurance, you may be among the many who are looking forward hopefully to marriage, and praying that God will bring the right partner into their lives. This waiting period can, if you are not careful, be a time of frustration and discontent.

Popular books, television programs, and movies are producing a deluge of material about love and sex. Even if you sidestep as much of this flood as you can, it is difficult not to be influenced by it indirectly. There are obvious dangers for the single Christian in all this—the temptations of illicit sex, for example—but even if these are avoided, there is another, more subtle pitfall for those who hope for marriage. You will find it all too easy, in today's world, to become preoccupied with thoughts of romance, love, and marriage long before God intends. This can be a serious handicap to your Christian life.

Suppose, for example, that God's master plan calls for you and your future life-partner to meet one, two, or five years from now. He has a program for the intervening period, a wonderful program, which will help you grow spiritually, develop your gift, and realize the joys of service. If you follow His guidance, you will be fully prepared for the marriage relationship when the time comes. You can also trust Him to bring the right person into your life at the right moment.

In this waiting situation, as in all others, you can experience God's best only by letting Him plan your life. If you try to keep one eye on God, while the other sweeps the horizon for possible marital candidates, He will not be able to guide you as He desires, and you will be in no shape to enjoy the good things He has for you now.

How does God want you to live as a single Christian if you are not one of those committed to a single life? Let me suggest a few guidelines.

1. Tell God, and mean it, that you will accept either singleness or marriage as He decides. This does not preclude your telling Him frankly that you want to be married, if this is the case, and asking Him to bring it about. God wants us to share our desires with Him.

2. Be open to friendships with single Christians of the opposite sex, but don't try to push these relationships toward romance. Seek friendships in group situations where you don't have to pair off. Keep your dating casual until there is indication that a strong attraction is developing between you and one individual and that the attraction is mutual. Seek and expect God's guidance in your friendships.

3. As early as possible in a Christian dating relationship initiate the practice of praying together. Ask your friend to pray with you, from time to time, about some practical prob-

pray with you, from time to time, about some practical problem you face at school or on the job. Be prepared to pray about problems your friend may share with you. Prayer will help to give your relationship a spiritual dimension. Later, if friendship changes to something more, it will be easy to pray jointly for guidance in your romance.

Don't insist on prayer in the first stages of a relationship, if your friend objects. As your interest in each other becomes serious, praying together will become important.

4. Don't allow friendships with non-Christians to acquire romantic overtones, since binding relationships between believers and unbelievers are not in accord with God's will (2 Corinthians 6:14).

5. Recognize that your present single state, whether temporary or not, provides a God-given opportunity for your spiritual development as an individual. Commit this period of your life wholly to God, and expect exciting results.

God's Will in Your Married Life

If your courtship has been conducted as described in this chapter, you will have already become used to communicating openly, listening to each other, and praying together. If not, it is vitally important that you begin these three practices early in your married life.

Your decisions after marriage will be of several kinds. First, there are individual decisions. While you and your marriage partner have become one, neither of you has lost your individuality, and you must each make many personal choices every day.

Second, there are family decisions, which are of concern to all members of the household. Not all Christian couples make these decisions in the same way. Their practices tend to follow one of three basic patterns:

1. The husband makes all decisions, though he may delegate to his wife the authority for deciding certain matters. The wife suggests, but does not decide. This approach is based on the belief that the "headship" assigned to the husband in Ephesians 5:23 gives him the total responsibility for directing the affairs of the family.

2. The husband and wife both participate in the decision-making process. However, the husband, as head, retains the "tie-breaking vote" in case of disagreement. Those couples who follow this pattern interpret Ephesians 5 in the same way as those above, but believe that the wife should have more say than is customary under the first arrangement.

3. The husband and wife take equal responsibility for decision-making for the family. In this case the headship of the husband is not considered to be a mandate for decision-making, but a call for him to exercise loving spiritual support as described in Ephesians 5:25-28.

I am personally convinced that the third pattern is the most biblical, and the one that most effectively promotes spiritual oneness in marriage. However, Christian marriages can function satisfactorily under any of the three patterns, provided both marriage partners are comfortable with the arrangement.

Finally, there are parent-child decisions. "Train a child in the way he should go," the Bible tells us (Proverbs 22:6). The job of training includes loving them, instructing them in how to behave, serving as good examples for them, and teaching them the art of making their own decisions in a responsible way.

The following are a few suggestions for making certain that God's will is honored in your marriage relationship:

1. It is important that each partner maintains a close relationship with God. You can think of Christian marriage as a triangle, with God at the topmost point and you and your

spouse at the lower two points. If each marriage partner is walking with God on a daily basis, the triangle is a small one with husband and wife drawn close to each other. If either drifts away from God, the triangle becomes distorted and the distance grows greater between you and your spouse.

2. Whichever of the three patterns of family decision-making is followed, things will go most smoothly if both partners are content with the arrangement and if the wisdom and opinions of both are reflected in family decisions.

3. You should approach each major family decision with discussion and prayer. Maintaining open communication with each other and with God is of vital importance. Follow the methods described in Chapter 7 in seeking God's will. The solution should be acceptable to both of you. If such a solution cannot be found, put off the decision if possible until agreement can be reached.

4. Begin early to teach your children how to make decisions and give them the freedom to do so within reasonable limits.

5. Recognize that God's guidance in marriage is a multipurpose operation. As you and your spouse endeavor to live for God each day, you clear the way for His guidance to operate. As you seek His guidance together, you will draw closer to Him and to each other.

QUESTIONS

1. In 1 Corinthians 7, Paul suggested that his unmarried readers should consider remaining single. What are some of his reasons?

2. How do the words of Jesus in Mark 10:29-30 also imply that it is God's will for some people not to marry?

3. In view of these scriptures, what should your attitude be toward young Christians who show no interest in marrying?

4. How can a young Christian be confident that he or she will not make a mistake and marry the wrong person?

5. What about Christians who have married without seeking God's guidance? Should they conclude that they have missed "God's best" for their lives? Why or why not?

6. What are some possible reasons why the Bible does not discuss how to choose a wife or a husband? Does this apparent omission mean a young Christian should not expect God's guidance in choosing a partner? Why or why not?

7. How can a young man and woman apply the promise of Matthew 18:19 to help them to decide whether or not to marry?

8. What are some items that should be the subject of discussion and prayer between a Christian man and woman considering marriage? How does romantic love fit into this process?

9. Why might God sometimes allow a waiting period to occur between the time a Christian thinks he or she would like to marry, and the time the "right" partner appears?

10. What are some useful guidelines that can be followed now by single Christians who are looking forward to getting married at some time in the future?

CHAPTER 13

Problem Areas

L et's consider several of the more common problems that arise concerning God's will. One of the many questions that people ask concerning divine guidance is: "Why doesn't God make His will clearer?" Given a choice, most Christians would prefer God to use the most clear and concrete of methods in directing them. However, as we have seen, He tends to guide in unspectacular ways. Why? After all, He could if He wished answer every prayer directly and dramatically. • One reason He may not do so is that use of special signals in guidance would not teach you and me the important lesson of learning to think like Jesus. There are also other probable reasons. • Suppose the Lord made a practice of answering all your prayers for guidance in a definite unmistakable way, say by dropping down some pieces of paper out of heaven with the answers written on them. You would save these pieces of paper, and cherish them, and maybe brag about them. You might even be a little unhappy if another Christian had ten of these written answers, while the Lord had given you only five. And imagine, if you will, what might happen when an unsaved acquaintance challenged you to show reasons for your belief. It would be so easy to trot out your collection of heavenly answers and silence him! In fact, the situation could be well described by a loosely worded perversion of Hebrews 11:1: Pieces of paper dropped from heaven are the substance of things hoped for, the evidence of things not seen, for by them people are able to live victoriously. See what could happen? You could be well on your way to replacing faith itself with something far less meaningful.

It is perhaps to keep you from the temptation to substitute experiences and evidences for faith that the Lord in His wisdom prefers to guide through a deft shaping of circumstances, and through the gentle influence of His Holy Spirit on your heart and mind. You will find that when God does give you specific signs, they are mostly in the form of small incidents that you can appreciate but can't describe triumphantly to your unsaved friends. God doesn't intend guidance experiences to be used as "proofs" of Christianity.

While you know that faith is the principle by which God wants us to live, the old human nature inside you may subconsciously keep searching for material evidence to support your beliefs. Like the Pharisees, you may keep looking for signs and may begin to doubt when you don't get them. The occasional accounts you hear of God's answering prayer in spectacular ways may only whet your appetite for a similar demonstration in your own life. He will give you specific guidance that may reinforce the faith you have, but He does not want you to build faith on the basis of tangible evidence. His special signs are usually rare enough that they really could be statistical accidents, as the skeptic likes to call them.

If you put your faith in God and live in that faith, you will become conditioned to accept all life's experiences in the assurance that He is working for good in and through them. Then your peace will not be dependent on signs.

Why Does God Allow Troubles?

A second point of difficulty for Christians interested in God's will is why God allows trouble to come into their lives. Like the concern with signs, this problem stems from a natural desire to have things as easy as possible. It seems to us sometimes that the Lord should use a little of His great power to smooth our way on this earth, and to make our circumstances more pleasant.

One answer to this question has already been suggested by the chapter on "God's School," where I pointed out that God may lead you through difficulties as a part of your learning process. A moment's thought will convince you that difficulties are inseparable from any program of learning. For example, one cannot qualify as an expert pilot unless he can operate a plane under the trying conditions of night, rain, and storm, nor can he excel in the study of mathematics if he cannot solve difficult problems as well as easy ones. In the area of spiritual learning, could the apostle Paul truly have mastered the fact that God's grace was sufficient for every need if he had not had the "thorn in the flesh" (2 Corinthians 12:7) to try him? And could Jesus Himself have "learned obedience" (Hebrews 5:8) without the suffering that the scriptures tell us was a part of that learning?

There are other possible reasons why troubles occur in the Christian's life. Trials may be necessary to keep you and me from falling into sin. In the example already mentioned, Paul stated that a purpose of his "thorn" was to prevent him from feeling smug and superior because of the revelations God had given him. Experience and observation teach us that the troubles which the Lord allows in the lives of Christians often have the effect of drawing them closer to Him, or bringing them back if they have strayed.

Finally, troubles come to Christians simply because we

are called to live in a world at odds with God. Jesus told His disciples, "In this world you will have trouble. But take heart! I have overcome the world" (John 16:33). Our natural inclination is to wish the world were not a wicked place, but that's the way it is, and there is little practical point in fretting about it.

Christianity, if it is anything at all, must be the way of life that comes to grips with the realities of the universe. Jesus said He came to witness to the truth, and everyone that was of the truth heard His voice (John 18:37). Part of that truth is that sin, ugly and rampant, has permeated the world's environment. The god of this world, Satan, uses this environment to the fullest in his fight against God's people. You would never learn how the Christian faith works if God were to shield you artificially from the troubles that the world brings your way, and He has never promised to do so. He has promised to sustain you in these difficulties.

God uses trouble to develop you in your faith. Suppose, for example, another Christian wrongs you. In doing this he certainly goes against the guidance of God's Holy Spirit. Doing wrong is not God's will for him. But if you are walking with God, you can be certain that suffering this wrong is God's will for you. God has used His foreknowledge of the failure of the other Christian to provide you with just the lesson in patience and grace that you need at this point in your life. In this example, the complexity of God's will becomes evident. An understanding of God's use of trouble will make it easier for you to bear such wrongs. As Peter told us, "It is better, if it is God's will, to suffer for doing good, than for doing evil" (1 Peter 3:17).

Balance

As is the case with some other areas of the Christian life, it is easy to go to extremes in one direction or another while trying to do God's will. There are those who are so impatient to be up and doing that they find it difficult to wait long enough to learn what God wants. They plunge ahead in Christian activities hoping that God is pleased with what they are doing. Such Christians may become active in highly organized Christian service operations such as committees, planning groups, and active evangelistic programs (all very good things if operated in His will, by the way), but are often lacking in the equally important functions of prayer, meditation, and study of God's word. If they engage in witnessing, they may "buttonhole" those they meet without waiting for the opportunities God's Holy Spirit gives them, and may often offend. They are like unskilled but enthusiastic carpenter's helpers who, in their eagerness, rush to bring boards and tools which are often unnecessary and which clutter up the work area. Far from helping, they may actually impede the work.

At the other end of the spectrum are Christians who are so obsessed with the idea of waiting on the Lord that they do little or nothing in Christian service. They are concerned that they may do the wrong thing and that their activities in Christian service may be "of the flesh" and not in accordance with the Spirit of God. Such Christians tend to think of themselves as simply puppets activated by the Holy Spirit rather than partners in God's service. They spend commendable amounts of time in prayer and Bible study, but become so involved with thinking about their own spiritual condition that they often find it difficult to engage in any active program of Christian work. Christians who carry this attitude to its ultimate conclusion will tend to become more and more introspective and less and less active, until they will hesitate to witness for God, give out a tract, or engage in a teaching, pastoral, or gospel effort, unless they feel especially and mystically led by God to do so. Like some of the ancient hermits, they can become so concerned with themselves and their own spirituality that they are of little use either to God or to their fellow Christians.

To avoid both of these extremes, remember that the great followers of God in both the Old and New Testaments were persons of decisive action and of prayer, and that God's word counsels you to exercise the same combination of patience and energy. The same God who tells you in His scriptures to "make the most of every opportunity because the days are evil," also exhorts you to "pray continually." By following all, not just part, of the scriptural pattern for the Christian life, you can be a useful and well-balanced Christian.

Wrong Choices

A final problem is one that often haunts Christians who honestly try to do God's will: "What happens if I make a wrong and irreversible choice?"

Worldly Christians seldom worry about whether or not they have lost some of God's spiritual blessings through making wrong choices. It is almost always sincere and spiritual believers who fear that, by failing to understand God's will, they will miss a turning point and finish up as "second team" Christians. Young people just beginning their Christian lives are often the most concerned. Is this concern justified?

The possibility of taking a wrong step, which has permanent effects, exists for any Christian. A young man backslides to the extent of experimenting with drugs that affect his health, thus making him physically unfit for the missionfield to which he later wishes to go. A Christian girl marries an atheist and lives a life of conflict instead of the life of Christian service that God had designed for her. In these examples it appears obvious that the individuals' decisions have made permanent changes in their life circumstances. Maybe you can remember an instance in your own Christian life when you refused the clear guidance of God. However, even in these cases we cannot say flatly that the Christian involved must, for the rest of his life, be satisfied with a second-best plan for his life.

You see, God doesn't reveal His alternatives. He never publishes His complete plan for a life, but reveals only one step at a time. We can never say with certainty what would have happened if our decisions had been different. Every Christian life, no matter how dedicated, is a mixture of good and bad, of truth and error, of right and wrong decisions. It is pointless to wonder whether or not God had a plan for your life as it would have been if you were entirely, totally, sinlessly yielded to Him as Jesus was. Since God in His foreknowledge knew just when you would fail to follow His guidance, and on what occasions you would succeed, it seems reasonable to assume that His planning took account of these failures.

There are examples in scripture which show that God uses even the failures of His people. A case in point is Jesus' prediction in Luke 22:32 of Simon Peter's denial. When Jesus told Peter that Satan wanted to "sift him as wheat," He was predicting the circumstances under which Peter would later deny his Lord (Luke 22:54-62). The concluding words of Jesus were, "When you have turned back, strengthen your brothers."

In denying Jesus, Peter acted contrary to what God wanted him to do. But Jesus knew that this failure would teach Peter lessons which would enable him, later on, to strengthen the spiritual lives of other believers. The two epistles of Peter are wonderful examples of how Peter fulfilled his ministry of encouragement.

God knows that you will fail Him, as all of us do, but He has foreseen each failure. He promises to forgive your sin as you confess it (1 John 1:9), and He has already planned your steps after you recover from your fall, on the basis of this foreknowledge. And the experience you gain through this failure may be useful in your subsequent service for God.

This is a comforting truth, but does not mean that you are not held responsible for failing to obey. You lose, in a spiritual sense, each time you turn from Him in any way. But you must leave to Him the question of how your life might have been changed if you had made any decision other than the one you actually did make.

Your job and mine is to live each day, and make each decision, as a new experience from God's hand. While you may speculate about what might have been, you are wiser if you will leave not only the future, but also the past, to Him.

There is, however, a kind of second-best Christian experience that God wants us to avoid. It is what comes to those who consistently refuse to put Him first in their lives. Paul called such Christians "worldly." They are the ones who continue to follow their own natural desires, and who remain spiritual babies for their entire lives instead of growing in Christ.

It is in connection with believers who in any given instance do not put God's purposes first in their lives that the phrase "God's permissive will" is sometimes used. This expression is simply a way of describing God's attitude in cases where, having made His will known, He nevertheless permits a self-willed person to pursue a contrary course. The story of Balaam, in Numbers 22, is an Old Testament example of this principle.

God loves such Christians, as He loves us all. To the extent that they will follow, He will guide them, and He often protects them from the worst results of their own selfish decisions. But unless they yield their lives to Him, they can never experience fully His intimate care, His presence, and His daily guidance. These individuals can truly be called second-best Christians.

QUESTIONS

1. Why doesn't God always make His will clear?

2. Why is it not good to think of your guidance experiences as proofs that the Bible is true and God is real?

3. What are some possible reasons why God allows troubles to come into the lives of Christians?

4. If another Christian acts contrary to God's guidance, wronging you in the process, how can suffering this wrong be God's will for you?

5. What is meant in this chapter by a "well-balanced Christian" in the matter of guidance? How can you achieve this balance?

6. What are some wrong choices that can have permanent after-effects?

7. What kind of Christians are most likely to worry excessively about whether or not the decisions they have made are right? What kind of Christians seldom worry about their decisions? What is a healthy middle ground to take with regard to the danger of making wrong choices?

8. How can the fact of God's foreknowledge give you comfort if you find that you have made a wrong and irreversible decision?

9. How might the biblical account of Simon Peter's denial help you to recover after you have made a decision you realize is wrong?

10. According to this chapter, who are the real second-best Christians?

CHAPTER 14

A Final Word

What you are being offered, when you become a Christian, is an opportunity to become involved in the most revolutionary and wonderful campaign for good and against evil that the world has ever seen. This campaign is Christianity as it is meant to be, rather than the pale, watered-down imitation that we sometimes see. God's guidance is the control network for this campaign. • This great program is what the Christian life is all about. It asks that you, quite literally, regard those things that contribute to your own ambitions and interests as rubbish, and be willing to discard them for Christ. It promises that, if you consider all your days and hours to belong to Him, you can confidently expect to experience to the full the presence, the love, and the personal guidance of God. One of the strongest arguments for the idea of total commitment on your part and total guidance on God's is the truth that God wants you entirely for His own. • At this point I can hear someone groan, "I can never do it. This kind of spiritual perfection is not for me. If I need to be totally yielded to God and completely spiritual to experience His guidance, there is no use even trying to do His will." The fact is that God's great work in the world is being done by imperfect people, on-the-job trainees, functioning in the power of His Holy Spirit. He wants to take you as you are and put you into His service. Certainly you will fail in devotedness to Him, but He will be patient in your failure. Certainly you will make mistakes—He expects them.

In short, it is your willingness, not your ability to follow Him, that is important. He will supply everything else that is needed.

Where Will It Get You?

One of the first benefits you will find in following Jesus is that He can remove the tension from decision-making. As long as you are concerned with what a choice means to you, to your plans, and to your future, you are likely to fret about the outcome. When the realization dawns on you that it is, after all, His purposes that are involved and His plans that are at stake, the pressure is off. You simply don't need to worry. The God of all the universe is working in your life, and He is not in the habit of making a mess of things!

A second result of committing yourself to God is that your life will be important in the only way that really matters. In every one of us there is a deep desire that life counts for something. But the Bible makes clear that true success in this world must be measured by the standards of the next world. Only by yielding yourself to Christ can you know what is "his good, pleasing, and perfect will" (Romans 12:1-2).

Living for Christ is an adventure that can never be dull or disappointing. Unfortunately, some of us have, through our failure to live for Him, succeeded in so obscuring the dynamic image of Christianity that it may appear to others as a pattern of conservative thinking, compulsive church-going, external righteousness, and not much else. Christianity, totally lived and fully followed, is much more likely to create lives that are radical, in a true Christian sense, rather than conservative.

Doing Your Own Thing

The path God will lead you into will be uniquely, delightfully, your own. It is true that if you give your life to God you no longer live for yourself, but this does not mean that you will be required to become a replica of someone else. If you are a young person, God is not going to force you into the mold of an older generation, not only because the older generation probably does not provide the degree of spiritual dedication that He wants to develop in you, but also because it is important that you serve Him in the framework and environment of your own generation. You can't do that if you're a fossil left over from the last one.

Whatever generation we belong to, you and I each have one life to live. If we live for Christ, under His direction and where He has placed us, the result of following His guidance will be a happy life—and much more. It will be a life that will prove, in the light of eternity, to have made its contribution to God's great, eternal plan.

To begin living this kind of life, you need only say yes to God.

QUESTIONS

1. What is the great campaign in which God wants to enroll you? How does divine guidance fit into this program?

2. What sort of price must you pay if you want to be a truly effective member of God's campaign?

3. Why is your willingness to serve God more important than your ability to do so?

4. What are two benefits you will receive if you commit yourself fully to God?

5. Why do some Christians become tense and worried about making decisions? How can understanding God's program of guidance help to relieve this tension?

6. What standards does the text suggest you use in judging success in this world?

7. What lifestyle, practiced by certain Christians, obscures the true meaning of Christianity? What steps can you take to avoid this kind of superficial living?

8. Why is it likely that God will guide you to do some things differently from Christians of previous generations?

9. How can you make certain that your life will make a meaningful contribution to God's program for the world today?

10. Has reading this book encouraged you to make any change in your life? If so, indicate one way in which you intend to change.

Spiritual Gift Questionnaire

This appendix contains a questionnaire, or more accurately, a self-inventory, which may help you find your spiritual gift and use it for God. It will not tell you what your gift is. If you have read the chapter on gifts in this book, you know that you cannot discover your gift through a paper-and-pencil drill. The most that can be expected from this sort of inventory is that it will suggest the area of ministry in which your gift may lie. • The idea behind the questionnaire is a simple one. If the gift God has for you is one of the seven that are listed in Romans 12, it is likely that your natural abilities and your past experiences in the Christian life will bear a relationship to your gift, and will have been designed to help in fitting you to exercise it. In addition, it is probable that God has given you a positive interest in the kind of service that your gift represents. Part 1 of the questionnaire allows you to check your capabilities, experiences, and Christian interests against the characteristics of these seven gifts. • Part 2 of the questionnaire deals with those gifts that are not listed in Romans 12 but appear in the Corinthian and Ephesian passages. In Chapter 9 of this book, I identified eight such gifts. I also showed that they differ in kind from those in Romans 12, and that they tend to become active as God brings about, in each person's life, circumstances appropriate to their use. Part 2 has been designed accordingly.

In the questionnaire you will be asked to score yourself against a series of statements. For best results, be as objective as possible. There are no "right" or "wrong" answers. The variation in your scores from one statement to the next is the means by which your qualifications for one area of service will become clear. Since none of us can be completely objective about himself, it might be helpful, after you have gone through this exercise, to have a close Christian friend—one who knows you well—evaluate you, using the questionnaire, and then compare your results with your friend's.

A word of caution is also in order. If you have only recently accepted Christ as your Savior, you have not had a chance to experience God's leading in your life over a period of time. Under these circumstances, use of this questionnaire would be premature and probably misleading. It would be better to wait until you are a year or so into the Christian life before doing this exercise.

How to Fill Out the Questionnaire

On a blank sheet of paper, make an answer sheet similar to that shown below. Read each of the statements in the questionnaire. Decide in each case the extent to which the statement is true of you. Record the results after the appropriate number on the answer sheet, using the following scoring system:

"4" — The statement is completely true of you, or true nearly all of the time.

"3" — The statement is generally true, or true more than half the time.

"2" — The half-way level. The statement is partly true, or true about 50 percent of the time.

"1" — The statement is true only to a minor degree, or true less than half the time.

"0" — The statement is not true, or almost never true.

To help in keeping your answers objective, it is suggested that you do not read the instructions for scoring and interpreting results until you have completed the questionnaire.

The Answer Sheet

Part 1

1.......	8	15......	22......	29......	36......
2.......	9	16......	23......	30......	37......
3.......	10......	17......	24......	31......	38......
4.......	11......	18......	25......	32......	39......
5.......	12......	19......	26......	33......	40......
6.......	13......	20......	27......	34......	41......
7.......	14......	21......	28......	35......	42......

Part 2

1.......

2.......

3.......

4.......

Questionnaire

Part 1

1. You are good at explaining scriptural truths to others, and adept in using illustrations to get across complicated ideas.

2. When someone wrongs you, your immediate reaction is to feel sad rather than angry or hurt. You are always quick to forgive and forget a wrong done you.

3. You are quick to see the practical tasks that need to be done in your Christian circle, and to do these tasks without being asked.

4. You have the ability to visualize the overall scope of a proposed Christian project and enjoy planning such projects.

5. You go out of your way to spend time with Christians whom others seem to neglect, such as elderly, shy, or unsociable persons.

6. You are good at handling and saving money.

7. You usually prefer to read scripture for its immediate spiritual impact, rather than to concern yourself with the precise meaning of its words and sentences.

8. You enjoy presenting material before groups, but it is important to you to have prepared your material thoroughly beforehand.

9. You feel strong sympathy for those who fall into sin, even when the sins they commit could be considered by many to be inexcusable.

10. You would rather serve as a member of a project team than organize or direct the project.

11. You enjoy being given the responsibility for directing a Christian project; you can set goals and schedules for such a project and stick to them.

12. You are faithful in visiting sick friends and find pleasure and fulfillment in knowing that your visit has cheered them.

13. You are deeply interested in the financial support of the Lord's work, and you try, before giving, to determine which causes are most worthy of support.

14. You enjoy speaking before groups, and you would much rather talk spontaneously and informally than give a prepared speech.

15. When given an hour to spend with your Bible, you more often choose to study a passage or topic rather than to read for immediate practical application.

16. You can sense when others are unhappy or troubled and are strongly drawn to those in this condition.

17. You would usually rather do a job yourself than explain to someone else how to do it.

18. When directing a team project, you try to delegate parts of the responsibility to others in accordance with their abilities, and you are usually able to do so effectively.

19. You are a good listener, to whom others often confide their inner doubts and troubles. You are discreet and never repeat these confidences to others.

20. You tithe faithfully and, in addition, give as much as you can beyond your tithe.

21. You particularly enjoy sharing with other Christians practical truths for daily living, which God has given you from the scripture.

22. You are usually able to understand both sides of a question of scripture interpretation, and you are tolerant of those who hold views other than your own.

23. You are able to express love and concern to those in trouble, not necessarily with words, but simply by being with them, and you find satisfaction in meeting their needs in this way.

24. In general, you prefer being assigned short-range, specific tasks to do rather than longer-term, complex ones.

25. You enjoy instructing others in practical tasks, and can communicate well in practical matters.

26. Other Christians seem to turn naturally to you for spiritual counsel and often act on your advice.

27. When you think of those in fulltime Christian work, your concern invariably focuses on their financial needs. You are strongly motivated to contribute to help meet those needs.

28. You consistently find, in your daily Bible reading, fresh spiritual truths of a sort that provide active direction for life in the modern world.

29. In oral or written presentations, you like to organize your subject matter in logical, step-by-step form, with no loose ends.

30. You will listen at length, and with patience and sympathy, to people who pour out their feelings of resentment, bitterness, or frustration, even if their feelings are unjustified.

31. You get a greater satisfaction from serving effectively in some behind-the-scenes capacity than in occupying a prominent role.

32. When working with other Christians on a joint project, you are often able to smooth out differences among your fellow workers and to help in improving the morale of the group in other ways.

33. You pray regularly for the welfare and spiritual progress of younger or less experienced Christians by name.

34. You find pleasure and fulfillment in helping to support the Lord's work through your giving, and you feel truly a part of the programs to which you contribute.

35. The scriptures you like best are those which show that God works actively in the world today, and that we, as Christians, are an important part of His program.

Special guidelines for statements 36 to 42 only: Statements 36 to 42 are designed to determine what types of Christian service you would enjoy most or feel most comfortable doing. Put down a "4" for the service or services for which you would feel most motivated, a "0" for those you would enjoy least, and score the rest in between.

36. Conducting classes for other Christians in the important doctrines of scripture.

37. Visiting those in prison, those in hospitals, or those who have been separated from Christian fellowship because of their sin.

38. Doing clerical or manual work as a part of a team working on an important Christian program.

39. Taking full responsibility for planning, organizing, or directing a Christian project in which you and others will serve.

40. Guiding and encouraging a group of believers who are younger in the faith.

41. Helping to arrange the financial planning and support for a new Christian outreach project.

42. Sharing with other Christians fresh insights God has given you from scripture that you feel will give them practical guidance for daily living.

Part 2

1. You have, during your Christian life, been placed in circumstances where you have repeatedly had to demonstrate personal faith and trust in God to an unusual degree. The unique quality of your faith is recognized by other Christians and has been an inspiration to them. You are motivated to devote yourself to a Christian service where special faith is a daily necessity.

2. You have, during your Christian life, been brought into confrontation with subtle and powerful satanic teachings in a way that most Christians have not experienced. You have been given an ability by the Holy Spirit to discern and expose these teachings, and your discernment has helped other Christians to understand the danger of these teachings. You are motivated to devote yourself to combating false teaching.

3. You have, during your Christian life, been placed in circumstances where you have been used by the Lord to start one or more new church testimonies. You have been the catalyst around whom the new church grew. You are motivated to devote yourself to a ministry of founding new churches.

4. You have, during your Christian life, been used more frequently than other Christians of your acquaintance to bring uncommitted persons to the point of accepting Christ as Savior. You have a burning desire to see people saved. Other Christians recognize your capability and bring individuals to you so that you may speak to them about their salvation.

How to Compute Your Score

When you have filled out both parts of the answer sheet, you are ready to determine your score totals. Add the numbers (across each horizontal row) for Part 1, and write the total at the end of the row (that is, add the scores you have put down for statements 1, 8, 15, 22, 29, and 36 to obtain the total for the first row, and so on). After recording these totals, write in the names of the gifts for Part 1 next to the totals in the following order:

For horizontal row 1: teaching
                               2: showing mercy
                               3: serving
                               4: leading
                               5: encouraging (pastoring)
                               6: giving
                               7: prophesying

For Part 2, no addition is necessary, since each of the numbered statements applies to a different gift. Write in the names of the Part 2 gifts after your scores for the four statements in the following order:

After statement No. 1: faith
                               2: discerning of spirits
                               3: apostleship
                               4: evangelism

If I had included the miraculous "sign" gifts in this questionnaire, they would have found their place in Part 2. I have omitted them for two reasons: first, as stated earlier, I seriously doubt that these gifts are in general use today; second, since according to the Bible record the power to work miracles seems to have come on individuals in sudden, and sometimes unexpected fashion, there would appear to be little merit in trying to use a questionnaire technique to discover such a gift.

Interpreting the Results

Since its original development, versions of this questionnaire have been used by Christians of various ages and degrees of spiritual maturity. In some cases, the results have pointed clearly to a specific gift; in other cases, high scores were registered for several gifts, among which the individual concerned has subsequently found his or her own.

To interpret your own results, circle those gifts in Part 1 of the answer sheet that show the highest scores. If you have a sharp break in scores between the two highest gifts and all the rest, circle the two highest. If you have three or four scores that are higher than the rest, mark them. The gifts with the highest scores define the areas of service in which your present aptitudes and interests lie. If you have scored a 3 or a 4 on one of the Part 2 statements, your gift may lie in that area. If you have scored high on one or more gifts in Part 1 as well as on a Part 2 gift, you should keep both possibilities open until God guides you in one direction or the other.

What Next?

On the basis of your questionnaire results, you are now in a position to concentrate more of your thought and effort on specific areas of Christian service. Ask God to open doors for you in these areas, and to make clear to you whether or not you are on the right track (the steps in this process have been outlined in Chapter 10). Discuss your progress from time to time with a trusted Christian counselor, and look for positive spiritual results in your life.

If your questionnaire scores show no high points in either Part 1 or Part 2, don't be concerned. This probably means only that the direction which your Christian service is to take is not yet developed in your life. More time is needed.

As you study the scriptures and serve the Lord in whatever He gives you to do, you will learn where your gift lies. For the time being, you should concentrate on all the types of service listed in Part 1. Try the questionnaire again at a later stage in your Christian experience.

What may those of you whose questionnaires have yielded positive results expect from the future? If for any reason the results of this exercise send you in a wrong direction, you may expect that the Lord will quickly correct it as you look to Him for guidance in your service. Otherwise, He will reinforce what the questionnaire has shown, and refine your understanding so that you will be able to identify your specific gift.

As you become sure of your gift, you will have greater freedom in using it as well as greater responsibility to see that it is employed for God's glory. Concentrating on using your gift can sometimes involve turning down other good but time-consuming activities that well-intentioned Christian friends urge on you. Your refusal may be misunderstood. But if your purpose is to do for God the special kind of service for which He has fitted you, you will find peace and a more than adequate reward.

Notes

1. Divine Foreknowledge and Predestination

The question of what God's foreknowledge is, and how He uses it, is part of a centuries-old debate about divine sovereignty and human free will. While the words *predestination* and *foreknowledge* as used in Romans 8 do not directly concern our salvation, but rather our being conformed to the image of Christ, the passage establishes a relationship between these important words, and thus colors our view of how God operates.

Calvinists teach that we become Christians and are subsequently conformed to His image because God has chosen us, and that human decision plays little or no part in either process. They believe that as God sees an event in the future He simultaneously determines that it will take place. The result is that *foreknowledge* and *predestination* mean almost the same thing (see Chafer VII, 158-159).

At the opposite end of the spectrum is Wesleyan Arminianism, which teaches that human free will prevails in all decisions involving the individual destinies of men and women.

Many who would not classify themselves as Calvinists believe Arminianism goes too far in the other direction. These Christians recognize God's sovereign right to determine the fate of each individual. They believe also that God has, in grace, given human beings a free will. They further believe there is a divinely ordained balance between these two truths. This stance, which falls between the two extremes, is the one taken in this book.

The analysis of Romans 8:28-29 by the Swiss theologian,

Frederic Godet, was consistent with this view. He pointed out that the Greek word *foreknow* in other biblical and secular uses does not carry the special meaning assigned to it by Calvinists, but consistently means "to know in advance." He also stated that the series of verbs—*foreknew, predestined, called, justified, glorified*—form a chain of gradation where a contrast between successive terms is clearly implied. The grammar in both Greek and English is destroyed if there is no progression of meaning from *foreknew* to *predestined*—that is, if both terms mean essentially the same thing. Godet concluded:

> We thus get at the thought of the apostle: whom God knew beforehand as certain to believe, whose faith He beheld eternally, He designated, *predestined*, as the objects of a grand decree, to wit that He will not abandon them till He has brought them to the perfect likeness of His own Son (Romans 325).

Godet's reasoning can be applied with equal force to 1 Peter 1:2, where Christians are described as having been "chosen according to the foreknowledge of God the Father." His view of this admittedly complex matter seems to me to be the most reasonable.

2. Differences in Bible Interpretation

Young Christians in particular are sometimes disturbed by theological differences among believers, such as the diverse views about divine guidance that are discussed in this book. Why do such differences exist among intelligent Christians who worship the same God, read the same Bible, and are guided by the same Holy Spirit? The following comments may be helpful.

God has made the great truths of the faith (the divinity

of Christ, salvation by faith, the reality of life after death, etc.) crystal clear in His word. Matters, which while important are less basic, are often not as definitely spelled out. In these cases competent scholars sometimes see things differently. This comes about because, regardless of our learning or lack of it, we are all finite people, dealing with the infinite word of God.

If we understand this, we need not allow differences to divide us. We should be tolerant of the views of others and learn from them, but study to reach our own conclusions. A. E. Horton's excellent paper, "The Teaching, Interpretation and Application of Scripture," listed in the bibliography, is suggested as further reading on this subject.

3. Did Apostles and Prophets Vanish with the Apostolic Age?

The statement in Ephesians 2:20, that Christians are "built on the foundation of the apostles and prophets," is the principal basis for belief given by those who teach that these gifts have terminated. In this book, I have taken a different position.

The verse does not say that the ministries of apostles and prophets were to cease but only that they formed a foundation for the church. Office buildings are built on concrete foundations, but this does not preclude builders from using concrete in upper walls and floors as well. The fact that the ministries of apostles and prophets were foundational does not necessarily limit them to that time period.

Prophets were active in the New Testament church. While they made predictions on occasion, it appears their broader ministry was less "foretelling" than "forthtelling,"—applying God's truth to current situations in a timely and practical way. 1 Corinthians 14:3 states about prophecy that it provides "strengthening, encouragement and comfort" for God's people. While the requirement for predictive prophecy undoubtedly faded as the New Testament scriptures came into use, the need for "forth-telling" prophecy is still with us. The view taken in this book is that presentday prophets, using God's word as a resource, meet this need.

The matter of presentday apostles is more complex. The original twelve apostles were appointed by Christ and were not replaced by others when they died (except for Judas, whose place was taken by Matthias). Peter used the word *episkope*, meaning "overseership," in relationship to Matthias's apostleship (Acts 1:20), and it is not inappropriate to consider this type of apostleship as an office. But there are also references to other apostles who were not of the "twelve."

Nathan Smith, in his master's thesis for Dallas Theological Seminary, "Apostolicity of Timothy and Titus," argued convincingly that there were two kinds of apostles. He saw a sharp distinction between the apostles of Jesus and those who, according to 1 Corinthians 12, were given the gift of apostle. The twelve, Smith pointed out, were appointed by Jesus during His earthly ministry and before His crucifixion (Mark 3:13-19). The gift of apostle on the other hand, together with other postpentecostal gifts, was dispensed by Christ after His resurrection (Ephesians 4:7-11), and assigned to individuals by the Holy Spirit (1 Corinthians 12).

Smith's view is consistent with references in the book of Acts and the epistles to individuals other than the twelve as apostles. In addition to Paul (who may well have been a special case), these persons include Barnabas (Acts 14:14), James the Lord's brother (Galatians 1:19), Timothy and Silas (1 Thessalonians 2:6 considered with 1:1), and possibly Andronicus and Junia (Romans 16:7). Smith held that there was a considerable company of gifted apostles in the early church (37-40). F. F. Bruce, in his commentary of the book of Acts, took a similar position (Acts 278). Presumably those gifted apostles carried on the original apostles' work of establishing congregations of believers.

In this book I have assumed that the gift of apostle is active today, and resident in those with a special calling to plant and nourish new churches.

4. Does the Bible State that Miracle Gifts Have Ceased?

The view presented in chapter 9 of this book is that the four "miracle" gifts or "sign" gifts are not in general use today. The question to be considered in this note is whether or not there is biblical evidence that they have ceased. Some believe such evidence is found in 1 Corinthians 13:8-10. The words, "When perfection comes, the imperfect disappears" (verse 10), are taken to mean that when the canon of the New Testament was completed, near the end of the apostolic age, God no longer employed miraculous signs.

This interpretation of the passage is not, as I see it, the most probable one. It seems unlikely that Paul would have inserted into the grand paean of love (1 Corinthians 13) a doctrinal teaching about the precise time for the cessation of gifts. Moreover, there is an alternate and simpler interpretation. It considers verses 8-12 as a unit in which earlier statements are explained by later ones. Paul's purpose, according to this interpretation, is to assure us that the present imperfect elements of prophecy, tongues, and knowledge will someday be replaced by perfect comprehension and face-to-face communication when Christ appears.

This latter view is the one taken by this book, and is supported by a number of scholars. F. F. Bruce wrote, "When the perfect comes at the parousia of Christ . . . the imperfect will pass away" (Corinthians 128). Frederic Godet stated that prophecy, tongues, and knowledge would be abolished "with the advent of the perfect state; consequently with Christ's glorious coming" (Corinthians 250). G. Coleman Luck commented, "Prophecy, tongues, spiritual knowledge will finally 'be done away' when the Lord returns in the fulness of His glory" (103).

5. The Gifts of Pastor and Teacher

Some link these two gifts together into a combined pastor/teacher gift. They justify this by applying a grammatical principle known as the Granville Sharp rule to the list of gifts in Ephesians 4:11. The King James version provides a fairly literal translation of this verse: "And he [Christ] gave some apostles, some prophets, some evangelists, and some pastors and teachers."

If this sentence had originally been written in English, we would find it reasonable to conclude that apostles, prophets, evangelists, pastors, and teachers were five different types of persons. However, since Paul wrote in Greek, some believe the Granville Sharp rule must govern. They hold that omission of the word *some*, before *teacher*, means that pastor and teacher constitute one composite gift.

There are reasons to question this interpretation. Interpretive guidelines such as the Granville Sharp rule are established because they are found to hold true in a number of cases. They cannot be proven to be invariably true. At least one authority, Thomas Edgar, has stated that Granville Sharp does not apply where the nouns are in the plural as they are in the above passage (325). I believe that Paul's intent in Ephesians 4 was to list pastor and teacher as separate gifts.

The fact that there is no support elsewhere in the New Testament for combining the gifts of pastor and teacher supports Dr. Edgar's view. The gift of teaching appears in the lists of Romans 12 and 1 Corinthians 12 with no indication that it is part of a combined gift. The word *pastor* (or *shepherd*) and its verb form *to feed* as well as the words *teacher* and *teaching* are applied to individuals in a spiritual sense in various other passages. In none of these cases is there any hint that the two qualities are linked together.

Since the evidence for a single pastor/teacher gift is so tenuous, resting as it does on a grammatical rule applied to a single scripture passage, I have wondered why the concept enjoys such wide-spread acceptance in the Christian community. One reason may be that it fits neatly into current church structure. In today's churches, *pastor* is the term used for members of the presiding clergy. It has become an office in the local church rather than a gift, and incumbents serve by appointment. Since pastors have the primary responsibility for teaching the congregation, it is natural to believe that they have been given a composite pastor/teacher gift.

I believe we are on more solid ground if we maintain a distinction between gifts and offices (see also Note 6), and if we consider pastor and teacher to be separate gifts.

6. The Gift of Pastor and the Office of Elder

Some believe that the pastoral gift is that exercised by church elders or overseers. Support comes from the fact that the Greek word for pastor is *poimen*, or "shepherd," and that elders are commanded to shepherd, *poimaino*, the church (Acts 20:28; 1 Peter 5:2).

However, the New Testament appears to make a clear distinction between offices and gifts, and I have felt free in this book to distinguish the gift of pastor from the office of elder.

Gifts are distributed by the Holy Spirit to individuals. Church officers, on the other hand, are appointed by the local church. A person's gift is not dependent on which local church he attends; he retains the gift and is expected to use it if he moves to another location. An officer of one church does not retain his position if he moves elsewhere.

The two church offices mentioned in the New Testament are elders (overseers) and deacons. They are responsible to create an environment within which the gifts that God has placed in that church can function effectively (though each elder is also responsible to exercise his own gift). The elders function in a spiritual capacity, the deacons in material ways.

At first glance, the biblical instructions to elders seem to call for the exercise of certain gifts. An elder is to shepherd the flock (Acts 20:28); to be able to teach (1 Timothy 3:2); to be able to detect and refute false doctrine (Titus 1:9). However, gift is not mentioned in connection with eldership and the sense seems to be that an elder should be capable of functioning in these ways without necessarily being gifted in them. J. N. Darby made this point in his comment on the qualifications of elders: "Gifts are not included among them unless the being 'apt to teach' might be so considered; but even this is presented as a quality—the man must have aptness for it—not as a gift" (Vol. 5, 145).

The view taken in this book is that an elder may have a gift of pastor, teacher, or distinguisher of spirits, but his eldership does not require one of these gifts.

Bibliography

Anderson, William F. "How To Know God's Will." *Letters of Interest*. December 1968: 8; January 1969: 8-9; February 1969: 26-27.

Arndt, William F. and Wilbur F. Gingrich. 1952. *A Greek-English Lexicon of the New Testament*. 4th ed. Chicago IL: University of Chicago Press.

Barclay, Oliver R. 1962. *Guidance, Some Biblical Principles*. Chicago IL: Intervarsity Press.

Barrett, C. K. 1968. *The First Epistle to the Corinthians*. New York: Harper and Row.

Baxter, J. Sidlow. 1968. *Does God Still Guide?* London: Marshall, Morgan, and Scott.

Blair, J. Allen. 1969. *Living Wisely*. Neptune NJ: Loizeaux Brothers, Inc.

Brisco, D. S. "That Still Small Voice Still Speaks." *Moody Monthly*. July 76:37-39.

Brooks, Cyril H. 1985. *Grace Triumphant*. St. Louis: Walterick Publishing Co.

Brown, Francis, S. R. Driver, and Charles A. Briggs. 1907. *A Hebrew and English Lexicon of the Old Testament*. Oxford, England: Clarendon Press.

Bruce, F. F. 1971. *New Century Bible Commentary, 1 and 2 Corinthians*. Grand Rapids MI: William B. Eerdmans Publishing Company.

———. 1971. *New Testament History*. Garden City NY: Doubleday & Company, Inc.

———. 1952. *The Acts of the Apostles*. 2nd ed. Grand Rapids MI: William B. Eerdmans Publishing Company.

Bube, Richard H., Editor. 1968. *The Encounter between Christianity and Science*. Grand Rapids MI: William B. Eerdmans Publishing Co.

Carlson, Dwight L., M.D. 1974. *Run and Not Be Weary*. Old Tappan NJ: Fleming H. Revell Co.

Chafer, Lewis Sperry. 1948. *Systematic Theology.* 8 vols. Dallas: Dallas Theological Seminary.

Christenson, Larry. 1968. *Speaking in Tongues, and Its Significance for the Church.* Minneapolis: Dimension Books, Bethany Fellowship.

Coder, S. Maxwell. 1946. *God's Will for Your Life.* Chicago: Moody Press.

Darby, J. N. 1970. *Synopsis of the Books of the Bible.* Vols 1-5. Sunbury PA: Believers Bookshelf, Inc.

DeWitt, John R. 1981. *What is the Reformed Faith?* Carlisle PA: Banner of Truth Trust.

Dobbie, Lt. General Sir William G.C.M.G., K.C.B., D.S.O. 1945. *A Very Present Help.* Grand Rapids MI: Zondervan Publishing House.

Eadie, John. 1955. *Commentary on the Epistle to the Ephesians.* Grand Rapids MI: Zondervan Publishing House.

Edgar, Thomas R. 1983. *Miraculous Gifts, Are They for Today?* Neptune NJ: Loizeaux Brothers, Inc.

Farstad, Arthur L. 1972. "Historical and Exegetical Consideration of New Testament Church Meetings." Doctoral dissertation, Dallas: Dallas Theological Seminary.

Flynn, Leslie Bruce. 1979. *God's Will, You Can Know It.* Wheaton IL: Victor Books.

Friederichsen, Mrs. Paul. 1960. *God's Will Made Clear.* Chicago: Moody Press.

Friesen, Garry with J. Robin Maxson. 1980. *Decision Making and the Will of God: A Biblical Alternative to the Traditional View.* Portland OR: Multnomah Press.

Gaither, G. 1982. *Decisions.* Waco TX: Word Books.

Gangel, Kenneth O. 1975. *You and Your Spiritual Gifts.* Chicago: Moody Press.

Godet, Frederic L. 1883. *Commentary on Romans.* Reprint. Grand Rapids MI: Kregel Publications, 1977.

——. n.d. *Commentary on St. Paul's First Epistle to the Corinthians.* Trans. A. Cusin. Edinburg, Scotland: T. and T. Clark.

Graham, Billy. 1978. *The Holy Spirit.* Waco TX: Word Books.

Grant, Howard J. 1976. *Knowing God's Will and Doing It*. Grand
  Rapids MI: Zondervan Publishing House.
Gromacki, Robert G. 1972. *The Modern Tongues Movement*. Philadel-
  phia: Presbyterian and Reformed Publishing Co.
Holmes, A. "Building on the Will of God." *His*. June 1973. 33:1,3,19.
Horton, A. E. "The Teaching, Interpretation and Application of
  Scripture." Appendix in *The Preacher and His Preaching*. 3rd ed.
  by Alfred P. Gibbs. Fort Dodge, IA.: Waltrick Printing Co, 1951.
Ironside, H. A. 1938. *Addresses on the First Epistle to the Corinthians*.
  Neptune NJ: Loizeaux Brothers, Inc.
Kelly, William. 1914. *An Exposition of the Acts of the Apostles*. 2nd ed.
  London: F. E. Race.
_____. n.d. *Lectures on the Epistle of Paul, the Apostle, to the Ephesians*.
  London: G. Morrish.
Lawrence (Brother). 1982. *The Practice of the Presence of God*. Trans. E.
  M. Blaikloch. Nashville TN: Thomas Nelson.
Leake, Thomas F. 1987. "How God Guides the Believer - A New Tes-
  tament Survey." M.A. thesis, Lanham MD: Capital Bible Sem-
  inary.
Little, Paul. "How Do I Know What God Wants?" *Moody Monthly*.
  November 78:103-106.
_____. "Lord of the Specific." *His*. May 1971. 31:16-18.
_____. "Missing God's Will." *His*. June 1971. 31:26-28.
_____. "So You Want to Know God's Will." *C.B.M.C. Contact*.
  August 1971. 16-20.
Loizeaux, A. S. 1945. *Use Your Gift for God*. Neptune NJ: Loizeaux
  Brothers, Inc.
Long, D. B. 1972. *What the Bible Teaches about the Gift of Tongues*.
  Toronto, Canada: Everyday Publications.
Long, W. Meredith. "God's Will and the Job Market." *His*. June 1976.
  36:1,4.
Luck, G. Coleman. 1958. *First Corinthians*. Chicago: Moody Bible
  Institute.
Lutzer, E. W. "The Compass That Points Up." *Moody Monthly*. March
  75:47-49.
MacDonald, William. 1956. *Christ Loved the Church*. Oak Park IL:

Midwest Christian Publishers.

Madsen, Poul. 1970. *When the Spirit Is Lord*. Bombay, India: Gospel Literature Service.

Matheson, Roy. "Can I Really Know God's Will?" *Moody Monthly*. June 71:44-46,48.

Miller, Andrew. n.d. *Short Papers on Chruch History*. 4 vols. London, England: Pickering and Inglis.

Morgan, George Campbell. 1978. *God's Perfect Will*. Grand Rapids MI: Baker Book House.

Mumford, Bob. 1971. *Take Another Look at Guidance*. Plainfield NJ: Logos International.

Myers, Warren and Ruth. 1980. *Discovering God's Will*. Colorado Springs CO: Navpress.

Nelson, Marion H. 1963. *How To Know God's Will*. Chicago: Moody Press.

Newton, John. "How God Guides and How He Doesn't." *Eternity*. November 1977. 28:40-41.

Norbie, Donald L. 1983. *The Early Church*. Waynesboro GA: Christian Missions Press.

Ogilvie, Lloyd John. 1982. *God's Will for Your Life*. Eugene OR: Harvest House Publishers.

Orr, Willam F. and James Arthur Walther. 1976. *1 Corinthians*. Garden City NJ: Doubleday and Company, Inc.

Packer, J. I. 1985. *Finding God's Will*. Downers Grove IL.:Intervarsity Press.

Pliny the Younger. 1963. *The Letters of the Younger Pliny*. Trans. Betty Radice. Harmandsworth, Middlesex, England: Penguin Books Ltd.

Richards, Larry. 1979. *How Can I Make Decisions?* Grand Rapids MI: Zondervan Publishing House.

Schaff, Philip, Samuel M. Jackson, and D. S. Schaff. 1891. *Encyclopedia of Religious Knowledge*, Vols 1-4. New York: Funk and Wagnalls Company.

Sears, Jack Wood. 1969. *Conflict and Harmony in Science and the Bible*. Grand Rapids MI: Baker Book House.

Smith, M. Blaine. 1979. *Knowing God's Will*. Downers Grove IL:

Intervarsity Press.

Smith, Nathan D. 1965. "Apostolicity of Timothy and Titus." M.A. thesis, Dallas: Dallas Theological Seminary.

Stanger, F. B. 1974. *The Gifts of the Spirit*. Harrisburg PA: Christian Publications.

Strauch, Alexander. 1986. *Biblical Eldership*. Littleton CO: Lewis and Roth, Publishers.

Sweeting, G. 1975. *How to Discover the Will of God*. Chicago: Moody Press.

Van Ryn, August. 1961. *Acts of the Apostles*. Neptune NJ: Loizeaux Brothers, Inc.

Vine, W. E. 1940. *An Expository Dictionary of New Testament Words*. Old Tappan NJ: Fleming H. Revell Co.

Weiss, G. Christian. 1950. *The Perfect Will of God*. Chicago: Moody Press.

Wilson, T. E. 1979. *God's Call to Special Service*. Spring Lake NJ: Christian Missions in Many Lands.

Yancey, Philip. "Finding the Will of God: No Magic Formulas." *Christianity Today*. September 16, 1983. 27:24-27.

_____. 1983. *Guidance*. Portland OR: Multnomah Press.

Yohn, Rick. 1974. *Discover Your Gift and Use It*. Wheaton IL: Tyndale House.

Zeller, George W. 1978. *God's Gift of Tongues*. Neptune NJ: Loizeaux Brothers, Inc.